500

Strangest Football Stories

500
Strangest Football Stories

Graham Sharpe

DEDICATION

To my Uncle George – a great early inspiration for my love of football,
who sadly died just as this book was being completed –
and his son, Steve, who can't help being a West Ham fan.

Published in 2008 by Highdown,
an imprint of Raceform Ltd
High Street, Compton, Newbury, Berkshire, RG20 6NL

Copyright © Graham Sharpe 2008

A catalogue record for this book is available from the British Library.

ISBN 978-1-905156-46-7

Designed by Fiona Pike

Printed in the UK by CPI William Clowes Beccles NR34 7TL

INTRODUCTION

Strange thing, football.

You must agree with me, otherwise you wouldn't be reading this, but did you ever go to a game when something a little out of the ordinary didn't happen?

It can be the most stultifyingly boring goalless draw between two disinterested sides, yet something strange will happen at some point. Whether it is verbal or visual you will always return from the game with an unusual anecdote to pass on. Part of the stand collapsed; the keeper looked like a reality TV star; a cat climbed on to the crossbar; someone told you a ridiculous fact about your new striker.

I'm a Luton Town fan – and it doesn't get much stranger than supporting a team that starts a season on minus 30 points.

On the very day I finished this collection of strange stuff about football I read that Roy Keane had just decided, purely to wind some of his players up, to change all their shirt numbers around. 'Players are obsessed with these bloody numbers and I can't understand why. We've changed some just to upset certain people. I like to rattle a few cages.'

I'd been reading a book about a man who had never played football at any sort of level in England but, having been trained as a spy, found himself turning out in defence in Russian League matches for Spartak Moscow.

I had just been told by a steward on the Orient Express train of the time that there was such tight security when Tony Blair and other high ranking politicians were on board that he couldn't use his mobile to find out how his beloved Arsenal had got on in a game. He told Blair, who then made it is his business not only to commandeer a phone to find out the score, but also walked all the way up the train to deliver the message to him personally that the game had ended 0-0.

If you have ever played any football at all, at whatever level, you'll have dozens of strange football stories – I've been red-carded for 'teasing' an opponent; booked for taking a phone call whilst running with the ball; worn gloss-painted orange boots before you could buy coloured footwear; thrown mud in the face of penalty taking opponents whilst playing in goal; seen team-mate Barry Wanless pull the net from the crossbar to allow a dipping shot to enter the goal and then convince the unsighted ref it was legitimate, to the fury of the opposition; subbed a player after two minutes for being so drunk he thought he was kicking the wrong way and persuaded another player that it would not be a good idea to stab the ref with the wrong end of a corner pole.

You'll doubtless be able to match these incidents from your own experiences, I'm sure.

But the fact that such oddities and bizarre goings-on are equally commonplace at the top level as in the Sunday League environment where I spent most of my career are what make them so irresistible and fascinating.

We may not be able to comprehend or emulate the lifestyles of the fabulously wealthy professionals of today but we can certainly look out for their pratfalls, puffed-up posturings and poncing about, and bring them down a peg or two by laughing at them and enjoying their discomfort when things go unexpectedly awry.

We can listen to those with a vested interest telling us what a wonderful 'product' top class football of today is – and then see with our own eyes the proof that it is often anything but.

Never forget that without fans and spectators, professional football could not exist. The game needs us more than we need it. Without us it is nothing.

And without humour and strangeness, football is less of an experience, not as engrossing. It is like the 'X Factor' without the nutters; horseracing without John McCririck; politics without John Prescott; the Rolling Stones without Keith Richards. It would carry on, but something, some essential ingredient, would be missing. That's why I have made it my business to catalogue and compile 500-odd of the strangest football stories I can find.

I hope you enjoy them – if you do, you must also be a bit strange – which is only good.

Graham Sharpe

1. ASHEN FACED

The dying wish of a fan of Spanish side Real Betis was that he should be able to continue to support his beloved team – albeit from beyond the grave. Rather than sprinkle his father's ashes around the Andalucian ground, his son decided to renew his dad's club membership and season ticket, and then take him to home matches in a glass urn.

However, this soon upset the club's security stewards, it was revealed in November 1995, who were concerned at the safety implications of the glass container. Officials suggested that as an alternative the fan should leave his father's ashes in the club's trophy room.

That idea was a dead loss, declared club cleaning staff who objected to the 'morbid atmosphere' it would create. A compromise was finally reached, permitting the son to bring the dad to games in a cardboard container, described as 'a sort of milk carton', which was placed on the seat to allow a clear view of the game.

'Every time Betis scores,' said the anonymous son, 'I give him a little shake.'

Opposition fans who heard about the fan took to taunting Betis supporters by waving milk cartons at them.

★ When Leeds fan Nigel Moss died, his widow, Wendy, arranged for his remains to be buried at Elland Road. When the box containing his ashes was opened for the August 2001 ceremony, it was found to be empty. Co-op Funeral Services were unable to explain where Nigel had gone.

★ Lifelong Millwall fan Fred Swann got a ticket for the 1999 Auto Windscreen Shield final against Wigan. He couldn't make the match – having been dead for the past five years – but family members put his ticket on the seat during the match – which Millwall lost.

2. THOUSAND-YEAR BAN

Trinidadian player Selwyn Baptiste incurred the displeasure of his local disciplinary authorities in 1955 after being found to have played in a cup match the day after officially beginning a two-year suspension for other offences. They increased his ban – by an additional 998 years.

* Manchester United striker Enoch 'Knocker' West served the longest ever British suspension from the game – 30 years – after being found guilty of being the ringleader of eight players who fixed the outcome of a United versus Liverpool First Division game in 1915, which relegation-threatened United were allowed to win 2-0. Knocker went to his grave declaring his innocence – and I supported him in my book, *Free The Manchester United One.*

3. TACHE THE WAY TO DO IT

One look at his moustache was enough to tell friends of Stockport County's dapper, 5ft tall, bowler-hatted 1906 boss David Ashworth whether they should approach him or leave him well alone when he returned from matches.

For the club's first ever Irish manager would wax his 'tache and when they won he would turn both ends up. If they lost both ends pointed down. When they drew it was a case of one up, one down.

* In January 1999 Eryl Southall, wife of Everton and Wales keeper Neville, told the *News of the World* readers that she suspected her husband of having an affair – when he shaved his moustache off. 'Whenever he had an affair, off it came,' the paper quoted her as saying.

✱ Liverpool, Real Madrid and England star Steve McManaman 'keeps a fake moustache in his car as a lucky charm' revealed *The Times* in 1999.

✱ Viv Anderson was the last moustachioed player to score for England (we're betting without six o'clock shadow man, Beckham, here, of course), doing so against Yugoslavia in November 1986.

4. THE BRIDGE TOO FAR

When Princess Diana's teenage niece and a friend were given tickets for a big Premier League clash between Chelsea and Arsenal on Easter Sunday, in March 2008 they booked a taxi from her home at her father Earl Spencer's Althorp Estate home in Northmptonshire to take them to Stamford Bridge.

The cab arrived and the excited friends jumped in and set off. The cab duly arrived, a mere six hours later, at Stamford Bridge, a village of 3,500 souls, eight miles east of York and 229 miles away from Chelsea's west London ground where Didier Drogba was scoring twice in a 2-1 win for the Blues, that is.

The taxi driver, obviously unfamiliar with Stamford Bridge's location, had put the name Stamford Bridge into his vehicle's sat-nav system – which sent him off in completely the wrong direction. Not that either he or his passengers appeared to notice.

It was not revealed which of the Earl's daughters – Kitty, 18, and twins Eliza and Amelia, 15, who spend much of their time in South Africa with their mother – was in the cab, but she could be excused for not knowing where they should have been headed.

The same does not go for the cabbie, who works – possibly worked – for Northampton-based Mayfair Taxis, whose boss Peter Achiampong explained: 'The fault was with the control staff, not the driver. He ended up putting Stamford Bridge into his sat-nav and it said it was in the North of England. He checked it was right and it was confirmed by the controller.'

Generously enough, Mr Achiampong said that the fare had been waived. An Althorp Estate spokesman confirmed the story.

5. DEATH PENALTY FOR MATCH FIXING

Uganda's Army representative football team was issued with a salutary warning about the consequences of match fixing, in February 2002.

'After acquiring military training, players turning out for the army team will face the firing squad when found guilty of match fixing,' declared an army spokesman from Kampala who told the africast.com website that this somewhat drastic warning was justified on the grounds that it was the punishment administered to any soldier found guilty of passing information to the enemy, and that 'that person has no difference with a player who fixes a match'.

6. DEATH IS NO EXCUSE

Amateur footballer Luigi Coluccio was given a one-match ban in November, 1995, for being sent off nine days previously in a Calabrian League match.

Club officials appealed for leniency but were told that the punishment would have to stand – despite the fact that the 23-year-old would be unable to serve the ban – having been shot dead by a gunman in Gioisa, southern Italy, two days after being red-carded.

'The posthumous suspension was unavoidable, since the referee's report was submitted before the shooting,' explained League president Nino Cosentino, in that caring, considerate way petty-minded officials tend to operate the world over. He added thoughtfully that the offence would also count at the end of the season when the fair play awards were being made.

7. THEY WENT TO THE CUP FINAL AND A PARTY POLITICAL BROADCAST BROKE OUT

About 80,000 fans, President – *check* – Jacques Chirac among them, were all waiting excitedly for kick-off in the 2001-02 French Cup final between Corsican side Bastia, and the already relegated Lorient.

Before the game got under way the French anthem, the Marseillaise, was played – but it was, not unexpectedly, roundly booed by the Corsican contingent of the crowd. Chirac was livid at this supposed insult to France. (The island of Corsica is a French 'territorial collectivity' and many there would like independence.) He demanded that Bastia officials should go and speak to their fans and apologise to the crowd.

He refused to permit the game to begin and called a press conference for the media, bemoaning the state of French politics. Only then did he allow the match to kick off – and Chirac himself was probably secretly delighted when Jean-Claude Darcheville of Lorient scored the only goal of the game.

8. DROPPED – FOR HAVING THE WRONG STAR SIGN

Former Arsenal star Robert Pires lost his place in the French national team – because he was born a Scorpio. French coach Raymond Domenech has always been keen on astrology, and in November 2005 refused to confirm who would be playing in goal for his side in a game against Costa Rica because: 'I consulted the stars. It was not the right day.'

Shortly before the 2006 World Cup, Domenech claimed he had problems with Robert Pires, because Pires was a Scorpio, reported *The Independent* newspaper's website.

'Domenech has a penchant for astrology and sees Scorpio as a negative aspect when he picks his side,' wrote *The Daily Telegraph*'s Rod Gilmour in March 2008, quoting a baffled and frustrated Pires, who had been playing really well for his club side Villareal as saying, 'I must be annoying him. It's like being at school. It's like I'm 20 years old and playing football for the first time.'

Pires duly dropped out of favour and lost his place in the team – while fellow Scorpio Bruno Pedretti also found himself unable to break into the side. Domenech has told reporters that he does not trust players born under the sign of Scorpio and tries to avoid picking Leo defenders because they are likely to be 'show-offs'.

Denying that he only used astrology to make team selections, Domenech said: 'All parameters have to be considered and I have added one by saying there is astrology involved.'

He added in a TF1 TV channel interview that astrology figured 'marginally, at the end of the selection process, when it is a question of choosing between players of equal ability'.

Domenech first admitted that he used astrology for selecting his squads when he was a club manager at Mulhouse in 1999 – 'Scorpios always end up killing each other,' he reportedly declared.

∗ Domenech was harshly criticised for the dreadful performances of France at the Euro 2008 tournament. Unrepentant, instead of placating the media and resigning afterwards, he publicly proposed to his journalist partner, Estelle Denis.

9. CUMBERNAULD'S CUNNING PLAN

Peter Murphy, a supporter of Glasgow non-league side Cumbernauld United, still recalls the time his club got hold of a genuine football legend to play for them, but decided to make a rather unexpected use of his talents.

'Cumbernauld took Kenny Dalglish on loan from Celtic, way back in the late Sixties. For a few, brief halcyon months they had at their disposal a player who would go on to become one of the finest strikers in the world, and an all-time scoring legend. So – where did they play him? In goal!'

There is, it is said, a picture in the clubhouse of a young Kenny up to his knees in mud, all padded up, between the sticks, looking bemused.

Whilst checking out this story on a Cumbernauld website, I came across another involving the club, now in the Stagecoach West of Scotland District League Division. In the 1914–15 season, Cumbernauld were going well in the Scottish Junior Cup:

'At the end of the drawn cup tie at Oban, the referee's final whistle signalled a rush by the players and officials to catch the last train back to Glasgow Queen Street and some players were forced to change on the Oban station platform before embarking on the return journey.'

It was only after the train had left Oban that one of the players discovered he had left his trousers on a seat on the station platform and he had to make a very embarrassing, trouser-less, journey home. Later a telephone call established the missing trousers had been recovered and they took pride of place on top of the Oban Glenmore kit basket the following Saturday when the team visited Guy's Meadow for the replay, which Cumbernauld won.

10. THE (GRAND) MOTHER OF ALL EXCUSES

Manchester City midfielder Stephen Ireland did not want to play for the Republic of Ireland in their September 2007 game against the Czech Republic. The player revealed that his grandmother had died and asked for compassionate leave.

But the initial sympathy for the player was tempered when his maternal grandmother, Patricia Tallon, revealed to journalists that she was alive and well.

Ah, said Ireland when confronted – you've got the wrong granny – I meant my paternal grandmother, Brenda Kitchener. Brenda read about her apparent demise and was so surprised and angry that she threatened the paper with legal action.

Ah, said Ireland – you've got it wrong again – one of my grandfathers is divorced and his elderly partner died.

Journalists went off to check again – and Ireland had to confess yet again that the story he had told might not have been completely true in all its aspects.

'I decided at that stage I must tell the truth and admit I had told lies,' he finally said. 'I realise now it was a massive mistake to say my grandmothers had died, and I deeply regret it. I would like to apologise to my grandmothers and all my family.'

Ireland then gave another reason, presumably this time the real one, for his absence, which was that his girlfriend, Jessica, had miscarried and that that had 'caused us to panic'. He said that when Jessica had indicated that she would like Ireland to visit her, the player, who was already with the Republic's squad, and she 'thought they might let me home quicker if they thought my grandmother had died. The manager – Steve Staunton – said there was no problem and the FAI hired a private jet.'

However, Ireland seemed unable to explain why he had not just told people about this situation initially, and why he also asked his club boss Sven-Goran Eriksson for an extension of his compassionate leave for their next Premier League game against Villa.

Eriksson commented: 'I hope he has learned a valuable lesson. Whatever your problem, keep to the truth. Don't tell lies because that is stupid.' One wonders what excuse Ireland might invent when someone close to him does actually pass away.

✱ In March 2007, West Ham's Anton Ferdinand told the club he had to visit his ailing grandmother on the Isle of Wight. It turned out he had flown to South Carolina for an all-night party at the Knock Knock nightclub.

11. SHOCKING

Never afraid to court criticism during his time at Chelsea, chairman Ken Bates not only suggested, but actually installed an electrified fence at Stamford Bridge during the mid-1980s.

Designed to deter hooligan behaviour, the maverick Bates failed to obtain permission from either the FA or the Greater London Council to implement his scheme and had to dismantle the fence at the end of October 1985, never actually putting it into action.

12. I'LL BE BULGARED

Hristo Stoichkov, the talented but temperamental Bulgarian front-man was signed for Barcelona by Johan Cruyff in the 1990-91 season.

'Stoichkov had a history of throwing tantrums and abusing officials,' wrote Barca historian Jimmy Burns, and he proved that when, in the year before he moved to Spain, his club CSKA Sofia had been beaten in the Bulgarian Cup final:

'Stoichkov distinguished himself by marching into the triumphant opposition's changing rooms after the final and smashing the trophy to pieces on the wall as the players celebrated in the bath – an act for which he was all but chased out of the country,' recorded Phil Ball in his Spanish football history, *morbo* (sic).

At Barcelona he soon distinguished himself by earning a suspension for stamping on a Spanish referee's foot.

13. BAPTISTE FOR LIVERPOOL? A DREAM MOVE!

Fans were buzzing with the news that Liverpool were set to splash out £3.5m on French World Cup star Didier Baptiste in November 1999.

The story was reported by the *News of the World*, *The Times* and Liverpool's own ClubCall telephone line.

It was only when it was pointed out that the player appeared to share a name with a fictional star player in Sky TV's soccer soap opera, Dream Team, that the media – and fans – realised that they had been hoaxed.

14. JOSE OUT WITH THE WASHING

Chelsea boss Jose 'The Special One' (as he dubbed himself) Mourinho faced a problem when in 2005 he was banned by the UEFA from having contact with his players during both legs of their Champions League quarter-final tie against Bayern Munich.

His punishment was imposed following a number of, er, indiscretions in their previous round's encounter with Barcelona.

When the home leg against Bayern began media pundits were baffled to see Chelsea's fitness coach Rui Faria wearing an earpiece, only partially hidden by a woolly hat. Was Mourinho issuing instructions through the earpiece, to be passed on to the players?

It was later alleged by both the *Daily Mail* and *The Times* that Mourinho had arrived early at the ground, and sat watching the game on TV in a dressing room, where he had delivered both pre-match and half-time talks.

However, knowing that he was likely to be spotted leaving the changing rooms, he devised a cunning plan to help him do what he wanted without ending up with a stain on his character.

Ten minutes from time, declared both papers, with Chelsea comfortably on the way to a 4-2 win, Mourinho clambered into a conveniently available laundry basket.

He was then wheeled away, out of the changing room, and off to the Stamford Bridge leisure club, where, it was then claimed, he had spent the entire evening.

When confronted with these allegations, Chelsea issued a statement, declaring: 'The situation is very clear. Both matches were controlled by UEFA and they were more than satisfied on both nights that their ruling was intact.'

Not what one might term a straight denial, you might think. Looks like Mourinho got clean away with it, then.

15. WHAT A DICK!

British singer Tony Henry was honoured with the task of singing the Croatian national anthem prior to the vital Euro 2008 qualifying game at Wembley Stadium in November 2007.

Henry had wrestled with his pronunciation of the words during rehearsals and was confident that he would get it right on the night. His singing was note perfect, albeit cameras spotted some Croatian fans in the crowd smiling broadly as he finished.

Henry, it later transpired, had reached the line 'mila kuda si planina' which translates as 'you know, my dear, how we love your mountains'. But as he sang he made a small error, actually singing 'mila kura si planina' – only a minor mistake, but one which turned the phrase he was belting out into 'My dear, my penis is a mountain'.

Croat player Vedran Corluka of Manchester City clearly registered the risqué version of the anthem, and smiled, even more so when they went on to win the game, Croats had nothing but praise for Henry, claiming that his error helped relax the players and calm their nerves prior to the vital match – one Croatian website even called for the singer to receive a medal of honour.

The publisher of Croat soccer magazine, *Torcida*, declared: 'It would be great if Tony Henry could join the Croatian team and fans at the European Championship – he obviously relaxed the players before the match at Wembley and if that's a winning combination, why not invite him to join the team to keep the winning streak going.'

16. WHAT A GAS!

Alan Hansen agreed to be interviewed by TV programme makers Zig Zag for a series entitled *Football Years*.

The former Scotland and Liverpool star turned TV pundit was filmed in front of his living room fire and paid a fee for his contribution.

But then, it was reported in January 2008, he demanded an extra fee – to cover the cost of the gas burned in his plush Merseyside home during the shoot.

Stories quoted a 'source' as claiming: 'A film crew went to Southport to have a chat with Alan about his years playing at Anfield. He was a very welcoming host and showed the crew around the house so they could choose a suitable area to film. They opted for the living room with Alan standing in front of the fire, leaning on his mantelpiece.

'He asked if he should put the fire on to make it look more homely and the producer agreed it was a good idea. They never expected a request for a top-up fee for his domestic expenses.'

17. PAULO HANDED BOOKING

Servette midfielder Paulo Diogo was so delighted with his part in setting up the 87th minute third goal in a convincing Swiss Super League victory over Schaffhausen in November 2004 that he dashed to celebrate with the fans, climbing on to a metal perimeter fence to do so.

The recently married 29-year-old Swiss-Portuguese failed to notice that he had caught his wedding ring on the fence, and jumped back down – leaving his digit behind. The game was delayed as he was treated and medics looked for the finger. But the ref was unimpressed – and booked Diogo for time-wasting.

There was worse news for Diogo as surgeons at the Zurich hospital he attended were unable to re-attach his finger. There is no indication as to whether his wedding ring was found and, if so, which finger he now wears it on.

18. OFFICIAL: WATCHING ENGLAND/SCOTLAND/WALES/IRELAND CAN BREAK YOUR HEART!

Men are three times more likely to have a heart attack while watching their national teams play in a vital match – which must be good news for followers of the home countries, as none of them managed to qualify for Euro 2008!

German researchers carried out a study during the 2006 World Cup in their country and discovered, according to research unveiled in January 2008, that there were substantial increases in the number of heart attacks and coronary problems when the host nation was in action.

The difference was so marked that researchers called for patients with a history of heart problems to be given precautionary medication before watching important matches.

Published in the *New England Journal of Medicine*, the report indicated that problems peaked on the day Germany beat Argentina in a penalty shoot-out.

'Apparently, of prime importance for triggering a stress-induced event is not the outcome of the game – a win or a loss – but rather the intense strain and excitement experienced during the viewing of a dramatic match, such as one with a penalty shoot-out.'

One might say this is research which should report directly to the well known University of the Bleeding Obvious – particularly as they do not seem to have compared the male response to that of females.

19. NEW BOSS BOOTED OUT IN TEN MINUTES

A 3.30 press conference at Torquay United in May 2007 unveiled former West Ham and Fulham striker Leroy Rosenior as new manager of the club.

As journalists quizzed the boss about his second stint at the club, the club chairman came and whispered in his ear the good news that a deal had just been finalised, with a Devon consortium to take over the club. He then broke the bad news – they didn't want 43-year-old Leroy as manager – he was sacked, ten minutes after taking over.

'Obviously they thought I had done a fantastic job after ten minutes and let me go,' joked the stunned Rosenior, who was placated by an offer of compensation after setting a new record for shortest reign as manager, previously held by Dave Bassett's 72-hour stay at Crystal Palace in 1984.

* Steve Claridge lasted 36 days as Millwall boss – during the close season at the end of 2004-05 and before 2005-06 got under way. They didn't play a game under him.

* After their first game of the 2007-08 season, an away 1-1 draw at Walsall, Carlisle United issued a statement – 'The board … regret to say they have lost confidence with Neil McDonald (the manager) and are terminating his contract forthwith.'

20. BROLLY GOOD

William Charles Athersmith, a.k.a. Charlie, was one of the very few footballers with the lavatorial initials, W.C., to play for England – which he did 12 times between 1892 and 1900, scoring three goals.

Before joining Aston Villa in 1890, Charlie played for Bloxwich Wanderers, Bloxwich Strollers and Unity Gas. He won the First Division Championship with Villa in the 1893-94 season when he notched ten goals for them; he won both Cup and League honours with them in 1896-97 and he completed his Villa career in 1900 with 269 games and 75 goals to his credit.

Charlie then joined Small Heath, for whom he made 100 appearances, scoring 12 goals. So far, so unremarkable.

However, Charlie has one football fact to his credit so peculiar, so odd, so absolutely bizarre, so smashing, that he is well worth his place in the upper echelons of this list.

Allow me to introduce a personal acquaintance, and author of the excellent *Corinthians and Cricketers*, Edward Grayson, to acquaint you with Charlie's claim to football fame:

'His feat of running down the wing,' writes Grayson, 'in a mackintosh in a League match' – hold on, it gets better – 'holding an umbrella, may never be equalled.'

★ In his book, *40 Years of Football*, published in the 1950s, Ivan Sharpe told how, during a vital Second Division game between promotion-chasing West Ham and Notts County in May 1923, 'a woman ran on to the field and assaulted County keeper Albert Iremonger with her umbrella because he was threatening to stand between United and promotion.' Hammers lost, but still went up.

21. ACCORDINGLY NOT SO BON

Every football fan is aware of the greatest ever winning match margin – Arbroath 36 Bon Accord 0.

It is one of the first fascinating football facts any enthusiast is acquainted with – but almost no-one knows much more about the game, other than that bizarre result.

I have discovered a contemporary report of the game, taken from the *Dundee Courier and Argus* in 1866 which is a little more informative – and closes with a killer fact that links the event to the extraordinary story above.

'This match – the first cup tie – was played at Arbroath on Saturday when, despite the rain, there was a good turn-out of spectators. The match was one of the drollest ever seen here or anywhere else, and baffles description.

'It was truly 'The Massacre of the Innocents' for a more helpless set of innocents never before met the crack club of Forfarshire. Though unable to describe the match, we can give the result, which we hope no-one will doubt. Two forty fives were played. The first result was Arbroath 15 Bon Accord 0; second – Arbroath 21 Bon Accord 0. Grand total – Arbroath 36 Bon Accord 0.

'Milne, the active goalkeeper of the Arbroath, neither touched the ball with hand or foot during the match, but remained under the friendly shelter of an umbrella the whole time.'

22. THE SECRET OF HOW TO STOP MANCHESTER UNITED – AND CITY!

Despairing managers who have wondered over the years just how to get one over Manchester United seem to have been missing a trick.

Had they consulted legal eagles steeped in the history of the Lancashire region of the world they just might have discovered that the answer was right under their noses – and has been so for the last 480 years.

Back in 1608, the Court Leet Records for the Manor of Manchester contain records of a law enacted on 12 October of that year, which declares: 'Whereas there hath beene great dis-order in our towne, wee of this jurye doe order that no manner of persons hereafter shall playe or use the footeball within the said toune of Manchester.'

So, if this law has never been officially repealed, it follows that the results of **all** of Manchester United and Manchester City's home matches must be void, and that they must complete their seasons in future without playing any home games.

23. UNEXPECTED CELEBRITY FANS

Former Russian president Mikhail Gorbachev is a Wigan fan, according to the club who, during the 1969-70 season entertained Russian side Metallist from Khartrov in their first ever friendly against foreign opposition, losing 3-2 in front of a crowd of 3,992.

   Gorbachev had not set off on his extraordinary political career at that time and was the club's assistant secretary. Afterwards, he reportedly declared himself now to be a 'Latics' fan.

★ In January 2008, with the US Presidential race reaching a climax, *The Sun* was able to reveal that Democrat Barack Obama is a West Ham fan, claiming that the 'US Presidential hopeful has been following the Hammers ever since a visit to Britain five years ago' when he met up with relatives who all support the team.

★ Not to be outdone, Obama's big rival Hillary Clinton was revealed to be a Manchester United fan, just like husband and former President. Bill.

★ Pope John Paul II denied being a Fulham supporter in April 1999 after a Cottagers fan wrote to him and received a letter from the Vatican assuring the club of his prayers.

24. COME ON REF, HOW LATE WAS THAT DECISION!

Sir Bobby Charlton was stunned to discover that although he believed he had had a perfect disciplinary record in international football, he HAD been booked while playing for England – 32 years earlier.

   In 1998 it was discovered that apparently unbeknown to anyone other than the official at the time, Sir Bobby's name had been taken down during the 1966 World Cup game against Argentina.

25. BADGERED REF SHOWS RED CARD

Referee Chris Foy finally had enough of the delaying tactics which were preventing him from getting the second half of the Fulham Premier League match against Aston Villa in February 2008 under way on time.

Foy took matters into his own hands and escorted the culprit from the pitch.

The trouble had begun when Fulham's mascot Billy the Badger persisted with his break-dancing display on the pitch as the ref and players waited for the re-start.

Nor was this Billy's first brush with authority during an already troubled season for his relegation-threatened club. He had already upset Chelsea boss Avram Grant by trying to give him a hug.

Billy apologised to Chris Foy – 'Badgers are hard of hearing and short of sight. Had I known he was about to blow his whistle I wouldn't have begun the break-dance routine.'

* Deepdale Duck, the Preston mascot, was sent off and removed by stewards during a March 2000 Division Two clash with Oxford United when he (Simon Nash) refused to leave the pitchside area. In 1997 he had been accused of distracting keeper Tim Flowers during a match when he conceded a goal.

* When QPR were taken over by new Italian owners in 2007 there was an unexpected victim of the new regime – Rangers' mascot Jude the Cat – a black cat, viewed as representing bad, rather than good luck, by the superstitious incomers. Desperate tactics, involving the spraying of Jude's coat to convert it to grey proved futile and the ninth of his lives was duly terminated in early 2008.

26. SHE'S THE BOSS

Carolina Morace, then 35, became the first women ever to coach an Italian men's professional club when Luciano Gaucci, owner of Serie C team, Viterbo, appointed the prolific striker – 105 goals in 151 appearances for the national side – to the position in June 1999.

'The macho world of Italian football reacted with emotions ranging from astonishment to mild hysteria,' declared *The Times*.

Law graduate Carolina, from Venice, was unfazed by the job – 'I see no problem in going in to the dressing rooms. Any talk about the dangers of me mingling with male footballers in the showers is absurd.'

Gaucci commented: 'What matters in team management is your brain power, not your sex.'

After two league games (other sources suggest she lasted a little longer) Morace resigned, claiming too much interference from the team owner, recorded women's football historian Jean Williams. She then became boss of the national ladies team from 2000-2005.

27. SHE'S THE PLAYER

In 2003 Italian club Perugia were reported to have made an offer to sign German World Cup player, Birgit Prinz, having already tried to sign Sweden's Hannah Ljungberg.

But in December 2004 Maribel Dominguez actually signed a two year deal for Mexican men's side Celaya.

The 5ft 4in 25-year-old who had scored 45 goals in 46 appearances for the national team was set to turn out for the Second Division outfit, only for FIFA to intervene to prevent it from happening.

'Mexico wanted to be a pioneer,' said Celaya vice president, Mauricio Ruiz, and Dominguez added that the decision 'caused me some sadness. I respect the decision.'

Several years before, in 1995, USA star Kristine Lilly played for the Washington Warthogs men's team in the subsequently defunct Continental Indoor Soccer League.

28. BELLAMY LEFT BOOKIES FEELING UNDER PAR

After Craig Bellamy and Liverpool teammate Jon Arne Riise were involved in a bust-up in February 2007, Bellamy allegedly took aim at Riise with a golf club, because the Norwegian wouldn't join in with a karaoke session. He was fined two weeks' wages.

Bookmakers William Hill thought they were on safe ground in offering 100-1 that the Welsh striker would celebrate if he scored a goal in Liverpool's next Champions League game against Barcelona by miming a golf swing.

Punters did not agree and Hills soon found scores of them queuing up to bet that that was just what would happen. It did. And Riise scored the second goal in a 2-1 win.

Hills finally totted up the cost of their decision to offer that bet, and paid out some £50,000, with the biggest winner a Liverpool-based customer who bet £50 at 100-1 and collected £5,000.

29. PSYCHO THE FIRST

Before Stuart Pearce was christened 'Psycho', there was another player who had acquired that nickname.

Mark Dennis, a tough defender with Crystal Palace, QPR, Southampton and

Birmingham, may have deserved it, to judge by what he told website www. truegreats.com, which asked him for his most memorable moment and was told, 'getting stabbed by my ex-wife'.

They also quizzed him about his funniest moment in the game – 'During a warm-up I told Andy Townsend I was going to hit a young Mark Hughes with a left foot drive. I proceeded to drive it straight into his face, and gave him a nose bleed.'

What about his strangest request from a fan? 'Signing a young lady's bottom – I won't say where I dotted the "i".'

30. ON YOUR BIKEY, SON

With two minutes remaining in the 2008 African Nations Cup semi final and his country, Cameroon, on the verge of their first win over competition hosts Ghana for 41 years, together with a place in the final, one of their players conjured up perhaps the most bizarre dismissal ever seen in the tournament.

A Cameroon player, Rigobert Song, was down injured and being tended to by the medical staff, when Cameroon's Andre Bikey decided to rush at one of the luminous yellow-jacketed paramedics and send him sprawling with a blatant shove in the back.

The referee, as astounded as everyone else in the packed ground, had no option but to brandish the red card and send him off – thus causing him to miss the final.

∗ Earlier in the tournament Egypt's goal celebrations in a 4-2 win over Cameroon baffled spectators as scorer Mohammed Zidan pulled off one of his boots and raced up and down, juggling the footwear from hand to hand until the rest of the team fell to their knees to salute him.

∗ When Zambia's Jacob Mulenga scored, his teammate began stroking his right boot – even though he had scored with his head.

31. SVEN'S BALLOON BURSTS

Sven-Goran Eriksson's Manchester City side crashed out of the FA Cup in January 2008 – beaten by a balloon thrown on the pitch by one of their own fans before the match!

In the build-up to the first goal of the game, the ball ran into a group of blue and white balloons (bearing the slogan, 'It's Just Like Watching Brazil') in the goalmouth, leaving City's Michael Ball struggling to get the ball clear, and allowing Sheffield United's Luton Shelton to nip in and score.

Bafflingly, although City staff had been complaining about the balloons earlier, their keeper Joe Hart had not cleared them out of his box.

After City lost 2-1 there was no offer by Sheffield United to replay the game – in a similar manner to the gesture by Arsenal boss Arsene Wenger who in February 1999, when his side took advantage of a throw in, which was expected to see the ball given back to United, to score a goal, insisted on the game being replayed.

After the City defeat at Bramall Lane the balloon went up again – as players discovered that watches, phones and £2,000 of cash had gone missing from their dressing room.

∗ Also during the fourth round of the 2007-08 competition, as Middlesbrough tried to take a first- half free-kick in their game at Mansfield, footballs began sailing over the stand, landing on the pitch and delaying the game. There was no apparent rational reason why this should have happened – but it was repeated later in the game.

32. THEY'RE ALL BENT: PM

It would create a sensation if Gordon Brown claimed that Scotland or England had thrown vital Euro 2008 qualifying games, although given the fact that neither qualified, there might be some sympathy for the opinion!

However, the Albanian prime minister Sali Berisha actually DID make such allegations after they lost 4-2 to Belarus at home and 6-1 away to Romania.

'Football shouldn't be represented by thieves who sell matches,' he stormed. 'I would prefer not to see any match at all than be shamed by these kind of performances.'

He also wrote to UEFA asking for the matches to be investigated. This did not go down well with the players. Skipper Altin Lala hit back: 'Maybe you should start coming to the stadium to watch us play. You don't have the right to make a mockery of our efforts.'

Midfielder Lorik Cana said: 'This is insane. We put our hearts into every game we play, but we have to be realistic, accept our limitations and learn to accept defeat.'

33. SOUND OF SILENCE

The one-minute silence held before Fabio Capello's first game as England manager in February 2008 had been arranged to commemorate the 50th anniversary of the Munich air disaster in 1958, in which 23 people, including Manchester United players, and a former Manchester City player, lost their lives.

It had to be cut short after just 27 seconds when, as *The Times'* chief sports writer, Simon Barnes, wrote, 'the minute's silence turned out to be 27 seconds of effing and blinding'.

Later the same week, Manchester United played Manchester City at Old Trafford in a Premier League game on February 11. There had been a great deal of discussion and concern about how well the silence would be observed, and whether there would be interruptions, and much had been made of the fact that former City keeper Frank Swift was one of the victims.

Some people had called for the silence to be changed to a minute's applause so that any interruptions would be drowned out. In January 2008 Manchester City's official supporters' club wrote to United warning that 'some supporters will show a complete lack of respect' and asking them for a minute's applause. It was reported that City had written to the 3,000 supporters who had bought tickets for the match asking them to 'uphold our good name'.

The silence was ultimately immaculately observed. United wore red shirts with a white trimming on the v-neck, bearing no logos, no names, just white numbers. They all wore black armbands, although skipper Ryan Giggs apparently did not wear his in the second half. City were 0-2 ahead at half-time and won 1-2.

34. KIRKLAND HOPING TO BE FIRED

Chris Kirkland, the England keeper whose dad, Eddie, collected £10,000 from William Hill in August 2006 after staking £100 at 100-1 on his lad winning a cap when he was in his early teens, told *The Independent* in January 2008 that when he retires he will join the fire service.

Growing up in his native Leicestershire he visited Hinkley fire station as a boy and he returned as a Wigan player to watch firefighters training in their 'smoke room', which replicates the conditions of an actual fire.

'This interest has always been with me. The passion has always been with me,' said Kirkland, whose interest is taken seriously by firefighters themselves and who was recruited by the Fire Services National Benevolent Fund to raise their profile. He was invited to present the Spirit of Fire firefighter awards in March 2008.

35. UZBEKS UNDONE

Uzbekistan won their World Cup qualifier against Bahrain by 1-0, but were left seething by the decision of Japanese referee Yoshida to rule out a converted penalty for encroachment – awarding a free-kick to Bahrain instead of ordering a re-take of the spot kick.

The Uzbeks appealed to FIFA, demanding that the 1-0 scoreline should be ruled out, and the game voided because of the incorrect decision, thus giving them a 3-0 win. FIFA almost agreed – but declared bizarrely that the game should be completely replayed.

Now both teams were upset, with Bahrain coach Luka Peruzovic, who might reasonably have been expected to be quite happy, moaning, 'I am not happy. I have nothing to be happy about.'

Well, he did when his side drew the rescheduled first leg game 1-1, then drew the second leg 0-0 and progressed to the next stage.

36. BERG BOTHER

It may be unique in footballing annals – a match stopped by an iceberg. Some 2,000 Greenlanders – over half of the local population – were crammed into the stadium at Uummannaq to watch the semi-finals of the Greenlandic championships in 2005, for which some of the players had had to travel by boat for a week.

The match was taking place on a sand pitch close to the shoreline when an iceberg floating past suddenly capsized – a large section of the ice hidden under the water sheared off, making the iceberg top heavy.

The crowd had to flee, many in boats, to avoid the mini-tidal wave. As a result the game was abandoned. Eventually the tournament was finished with Nuuk beating Ilulissat 3-1.

37. WEDDING CROCKED BY FOOTBALL FAN VICAR

Helen Warner and fiancé Robert Madeley had set their hearts on marrying at All Saints Church in Mickleover.

They had opted for the wedding to take place on October 13,1984 at 3.30 but were shocked to discover that it was out of the question – as the local vicar refused to marry anyone on afternoons when Derby County were playing at home.

The admirable Reverend Benjamin Crockett, 20 years a Rams' season-ticket holder, declared unrepentantly: 'It has long been my policy not to marry couples after 1pm on Saturdays when Derby are at home'

When Helen and Robert had made plans for their wedding the fixtures for the season had not been released, but Derby were duly handed a home match against Plymouth Argyle.

Helen, a regular at the church since she was four years old, was somewhat miffed. She appealed to the Bishop of Derby, and the Archbishop of Canterbury, but eventually had to opt for a marriage ceremony at nearby Ashton-on-Trent. The couple were duly spliced while the 70-year-old Reverend discovered that he was by no means in the black books of the Almighty, for Derby beat Plymouth 3-1 as he looked on.

* When he was Spurs chairman, Sir Alan Sugar dealt with a similar problem to the one above by rearranging one of his club's 1999-2000 fixtures so that he could attend son Daniel's nuptials, swapping Spurs' Sunday, December 5 game against West Ham, with a Liverpool-Sheffield Wednesday match scheduled for the next day.

38. FALSE EQUALISER?

With the referee poised to blow his whistle to end the April 1960 Danish match in which Noerager were leading Ebeltoft 4-3, the trailing side launched one last assault on the home goal.

The official, Henning Erikstrup, pursed his lips and blew loudly – only for no sound to be forthcoming, as his false teeth came flying out of his mouth. As Erikstrup desperately grabbed for the missing molars, Ebeltoft put the ball in the net for an equaliser.

Erikstrup found the false teeth, rammed them back into his mouth and disallowed the goal. Ebeltoft protested unsuccessfully to the authorities that the game was not formally over when they had equalised, but Erikstrup commented: 'I had to get them back before some player put his big boot on them.'

* During an autumn 2007 edition of Jeff Stelling's Soccer Saturday show on Sky, Paul Merson was waxing lyrical – well, as lyrical as he ever gets – about the Watford v Colchester match when, in full vision of viewers, his front tooth fell out.

39. YOU'RE HAVING A LAUGH, REFS!

An Italian Cup tie in October 1999 was selected for a unique experiment with two referees officiating in a game – each would take one half of the pitch as his own.

But the game, between Sampdoria and Bologna, was abandoned early in the second half – because of crowd trouble – with the 'chief' ref Roberto Rosetti making the decision to call the game off after Bologna keeper Gianluca Pagliuca – formerly with Sampdoria – was pelted by fans with fruit, bottles, water-bombs and, er, bath taps!

Bologna were leading 0-1 at the time.

40. HOW FA CUP LOSERS WENT THROUGH
TO NEXT ROUND

Darlington achieved a unique place in FA Cup history in December 1999 when, despite having been beaten 3-1 by Gillingham in round two, they went through to meet Aston Villa in the third round. Darlington were the beneficiaries of a very controversial decision by Manchester United to pull out of the tournament in favour of contesting the World Club Championship.

So a draw was held to nominate a 'lucky loser' to take United's place in the third round, and Darlington won.

42. ALLO LUV, WHO DO YOU SUPPORT?

A 2008 survey by Football Fans Census purportedly discovered that '42 per cent of men would never date a woman who supports their arch rivals.' Only 42 per cent?!

43. GHOULKEEPER

Arsenal keeper Manuel Almunia revealed that he believed his house was haunted by the ghost of a monk.

The 30-year-old Spaniard's wife, Ana, saw the spectre at their Abbots Langley, Hertfordshire home, which was allegedly built on the site of a former asylum.

'My house is small, but there is a lot of history to it, and it seems there are ghosts,' he told *The Sun* in February 2008. 'When we first moved in we heard strange noises like chains being dragged around. Then when we were sleeping the stereo came on at full volume.

'One night my wife suddenly woke me up with a shout. She said there was this monk-like figure with a candle in his hand. I was s*** scared.'

The paper reported that Almunia had been given permission by boss Arsene

Wenger to go home at lunchtimes from training to avoid leaving his frightened wife on her own.

* Arsenal used to have another ghost – that of former boss Herbert Chapman, who was said to haunt the corridors of Highbury. But he does not yet appear to have followed them to the Emirates Stadium.

* Two Sunderland physiotherapists reportedly chased a 'shadowy black figure' at their training ground, which promptly vanished. Striker Stephen Elliott also claimed to have seen the ghost, which was apparently identified by locals as an 18th century recluse known as 'Spottee' believed to be a harbinger of bad luck. Sunderland's next game, after an eight-match winning streak, on April 9, 2005 resulted in a 1-2 home defeat by Reading.

44. A MODEL DEATH

Liverpool fan Mark Taylor, 40, was so proud of his club that he purchased a plaster-cast replica of their ground, Anfield.

In February 2005 he fell on to the replica during an incident with a flat-mate at his Poole, Dorset home. The father of two suffered two broken ribs, a collapsed lung and extensive internal bleeding as a result, but did not seek medical aid for his injuries and died two days later.

A murder investigation was launched but there was not sufficient evidence for a prosecution. Pathologist Dr Basil Purdue told an inquest in Bournemouth that marks on the body matched a broken part of the model. The coroner recorded a verdict of accidental death.

45. SHORTS' SHRIFT

Iain Mills, director of Bury FC, resigned in February 2008 – after complaints about his regular wearing of shorts.

'He is concerned that his shorts have become a major consideration in connection with the club,' read a statement on the club's website which had readers checking that the date was not April 1.

'It is putting the board in an embarrassing position which Iain feels is not in the club's best interests,' explained the statement, confirming that he had stepped down.

The Bury board claimed that they were 'deeply disappointed' at Iain's departure.

Weighing in at over 21 stone, Mills was known for wearing shorts to games, refusing to conform to traditional boardroom dress of suit and tie.

'I thought we'd moved out of the Victorian era,' said Mills, a director since 2002, claiming that no club had objected, but adding: 'A small group of people have started to take exception to what I wear. On the rare occasions that I wear a suit the sweat just pours out of me. I am just more comfortable in shorts.'

Meanwhile, Newcastle owner Mike Ashley continued his habit of wearing a replica shirt to matches, apparently without complaint.

46. JEWELLERY JOKE BACKFIRED

The 28-year-old star of Lazio and Italy, Luciano Re Cecconi, entered a jewellery store in Rome in 1997 with fellow player Pietro Ghedin.

Re Cecconi, known as L'Angelo Biondo (Blond Angel), decided to pretend that he was a robber about to hold up the shop and steal its valuable stock, but before he could reveal that he was playing a foolish practical joke, the panicked store keeper grabbed a gun and shot him fatally.

47. I'LL SETTLE OUT OF COURT FOR $3 MILLION

David Beckham found himself the subject of a $3 million lawsuit, filed in 2007, which accused him of 'using footballs that are satellite-guided by James Bond and Pakistani intelligence to go in the net; dropping balls on the plaintiff from Empire State Building; receiving funds from Iraq and kicking them back to Buckingham Palace.'

Beckham probably didn't lose too much sleep when he learned that convicted fraudster Jonathan Lee Riches, 31, serving an eight-year sentence in South Carolina, had issued a – handwritten – $3m claim 'in British pounds' against him, which, if the former England skipper lost, would require him 'to wear the plaintiff's name on his shirt during all subsequent matches'. There wouldn't be enough room on his back!

Beckham was in good company though, as Riches had made other, bizarre claims against the likes of Mike Tyson, the Williams sisters and the International Olympic Committee.

48. DIVING ANTICS

Brazilian Marcos Paulo of Santacruzense got his comeuppance when he deliberately dived during a February 2008 state championship game in Sao Paulo – straight into an ants' nest.

'I only rolled on the grass for three seconds to win the foul,' explained Paulo. 'I got up, then started to feel sh*t. I looked down and my chest, side and legs were black. I was screaming, but the ref didn't understand and tried to book me. They were in my pants and right up me, so I jumped in a puddle, then ran to the showers. It hurt like hell. The players now call me The Ant.'

49. CATCHING HIS CLUB OFF-SIDE

Just what teammate David Beckham thought about it is not recorded, but LA Galaxy defender Ty Harden quit football to devote his time to helping others in March 2008.

'It has been ingrained in me that helping others is something that we have been put on earth to do,' said the 23-year-old, the club's 2007 Defender of the Year.

'I have loved soccer for a long time, but I have always loved helping people and doing things for others. I just got to the point where I felt there is more that I can do than just playing soccer.'

Oregon-born Harden played 24 games for the club and was following in the philanthropic footsteps of his parents in his new venture.

50. NO, WE SAID THE REFEREE'S A ...

Italian referee Mauro Bergonzi was forced into hiding after awarding two controversial penalties for Juventus against Napoli, whose more extreme supporters decided to take physical revenge on the whistler.

Thinking they had found their man, they set about him, and beat him up, reported *La Repubblica* newspaper in March 2008 – 'A group of people encircled someone they thought was a referee, they tried to abduct him and continually punch him,' the paper reported a witness as saying.

However, the fans had picked on the wrong man – 'The only thing was he just looked like the referee, poor thing.'

Eventually, the man persuaded the thugs to stop their assault on him – when he was able to convince them that he was really what he had told them he was: 'A banker.'

51. WHAT A PANTS EXCUSE

Reading manager Alan Pardew had no doubt what had led to his side's failure to beat Wrexham in their December 1999 2-2 Second Division draw – 'We started brilliantly, but this pants thing destroyed us,' he moaned.

And this despite the fact that his chairman, John Madejski, had reportedly joined in as an estimated several thousand Reading fans made their displeasure over recent poor performances known by waving pairs of underpants around. For a, ahem, brief spell, the pants were really whirling as Reading fell 1-2 behind, having been 1-0 up.

The campaign had begun on a Reading website and the 'pants' theme arose to indicate that the fans believed that: 'Players Are Not Trying Sufficiently.'

★ Pardew had other problems to deal with at that time – like refusing to permit Liberian striker Mass Sarr to visit a witch doctor to cure an injury.

★ In early January, 2000 on Channel 4's *Big Breakfast*, David Beckham's wife Victoria told presenter Johnny Vaughan that he 'likes to borrow my knickers'.

52. SHOWERED WITH EMBARRASSMENT

Striker Eldridge Rojer of Dutch side Excelsior suffered an excruciating torn cruciate ligament injury to his knee in early 2008 – while making love to his girlfriend in the shower.

And the ambulance crew called out to his home to treat him after his girlfriend thought he had broken a knee, found the star stuck on the floor of the shower, unable to move: 'I was stark naked. My girlfriend passed me a towel to cover myself. I was in so much pain.'

Eldridge came clean about the incident: 'I thought it was better to be honest to the doctors and medical staff.'

* In March 2008 it was revealed that Manchester United star Darren Fletcher was knocked unconscious – by a toilet door, which fell on him and gashed his head shortly after the end of their Champions League victory over Lyon.

53. IDENTITY CRISIS

Ipswich striker David Johnson played for England in a 'B' international. He also played for Jamaica in a friendly international.

Then he told *Goal* magazine: 'My old teammate Mark Hughes (then Welsh boss) has called me up for Wales, and I am looking forward to a long career with them.' He didn't get one.

He was then approached by Northern Ireland but, in October 1999 was unveiled by Scotland boss, Craig Brown, as his latest international acquisition. Johnson then said, 'I am committing my international future to Scotland. I will play with passion and pride.'

Brown indicated that the 23-year-old would be in the Scotland squad for the forthcoming Euro 2000 play-off against England.

When Brown announced the squad, Johnson's name was missing. The embarrassed Brown explained that Johnson, who was born in Jamaica, had a natural mother who was English and was therefore ineligible for Scotland, despite having been adopted as a baby.

54. WHEN WILL THE TRUTH BE TOLD?

Imagine the uproar should Sir Alex Ferguson be thrown out of football by a mysterious FA committee, which rules that he has been guilty of improper conduct, but declines to elucidate on that decision. There would be a media frenzy and almost certainly legal action would follow as the case was taken to a court of law.

It seems too outrageous even to contemplate. Yet exactly that happened to a predecessor of Ferguson – J A (John) Chapman, United manager from 1921 until the day in October 1926 when an FA Investigating Committee, which had held three meetings, two in Manchester's Grand Hotel and another in Sheffield, released a statement which declared: 'For improper conduct in his position as Secretary-Manager of the Manchester United Football Club, the FA have suspended Mr J A Chapman from taking part in football or football management during the present season.'

Chapman quit, his career ruined, but no indication or explanation of the reasons behind this sensational statement was ever made public to this day.

55. UNITED FAN IN THE PINK

Manchester United fan James Henry Farrow had barely been expected to live long enough, but he would be attending the 1909 FA Cup final to see his heroes take on Bristol City.

The Advertising Standards Authority might want to examine the claims a little more closely today, but back then the makers of 'Dr Williams' Pink Pills' were plugging Farrow's story for all they were worth, advertising their product to spectators at the Crystal Palace, where the game was taking place and declaring that Mr Farrow had been 'doomed to go under – just a frail, hopeless remnant of humanity, so affected by paralysis that his limbs were useless and his spine was too weak to allow him even to sit up in bed'.

But now, miracle of miracles, boasted the manufacturers, Farrow would be 'the happiest man at The Palace, as active as any man there' and all of this purely down to the power of Dr Williams' Pink Pills. Perhaps the United players tried them out – they won 1-0.

56. CHEERS, BOYS – YOU'RE NICKED

East Fife celebrated becoming the first British side to win a title in the 2007-08 season when they clinched the Scottish Division Three championship with a win at East Stirling.

But as soon as they reached for champagne, local police stepped in. They had put the champagne on ice before the game and club officials took the bubbly into the directors' box to enable the players to open it up and spray it over their travelling supporters after landing their first title for 60 years.

However, the local constabulary took exception to this and endeavoured to ban the celebrations, threatening to arrest East Fife's directors, on the grounds that alcohol is not permitted in football grounds – much to the disgust of East Fife director, Dave Marshall, who said 'common sense has gone out of the window'.

A straight-faced police spokesman commented: 'Officers spoke to club officials highlighting the potential for glass bottles to present a health and safety issue.'

57. UNDIE INVESTIGATION

Norwich City midfielder Matty Pattinson woke up convinced he was late for training, reportedly jumped into his car, wearing just underpants and a T-shirt, and drove to the club.

En route he was apparently followed by police who believed he was driving erratically and who arrested him when he arrived at the club's training ground – to discover that there was no training scheduled as it was the day following their 2-0 defeat at Sheffield United, after which some players had visited a nightclub.

The Daily Mirror reported on March 19, 2008 that the South African-born former Newcastle 21-year-old was to be checked into a rehabilitation clinic.

58. IT AIN'T SO, JOE

England's greatest footballing embarrassment – and there are plenty to choose from – is undoubtedly the 1950 World Cup defeat by the US of A, in which the highly fancied squad was beaten 1-0 by the footballing minnows of the States, thanks to a header by one Joe Gaetjens.

However, there is an argument that this result should be struck from the record books, as Mr Gaetjens was not an American. He wasn't even an American citizen. Which makes one wonder how he got into their side.

Well, he was born in Haiti in 1924, son of a Belgian or German – depending on which report you accept – father, and a Haitian mother. He came to the US in the late 1940s and studied accounting at Columbia University on a scholarship, and soon made an impression with his footballing ability. The goal against England was the only one he scored in his three internationals for USA.

He had been selected on the basis that he intended to seek US citizenship, which was apparently all that was necessary back then – but he never did, and indeed the next cap he won was for Haiti in 1953.

Eventually he returned to Haiti where, in 1964, he fell foul of the evil secret police, the Tontons Macoutes, who arrested and took him away. It is believed that he was killed by a death squad.

It is probably too late to appeal to FIFA to have the 1-0 deficit removed from the record books on the grounds that they played a ringer, I suppose.

60. SWASTIKAS OVER IBROX

In 1938 the England side courted controversy by giving Nazi salutes before a match in Berlin against Germany.

Two years earlier in October 1936, Germany came to Ibrox for a match against Scotland. They brought with them Nazi flags, complete with swastikas, which were flown at the ground.

In addition, the German side wore shirts featuring the Nazi eagle, and their fans gave Nazi salutes before the match – but the Scotland team refused to do so.

Prior to the game, Scotland keeper Jerry Dawson had daubed a small moustache under his nose and pulled his hair down over his right eye, mocking Hitler.

Scotland won the game 2-0.

61. FORGET THE CUP FINAL, WE'RE GOING RACING

Rangers were convinced that they had been robbed by a disallowed goal in the Scottish Cup final against Vale of Leven in April 1879.

So, rather than turn up for the replay, the players instead went horseracing to Ayr, leaving Vale of Leven to claim the trophy by default.

But in 1884, despite reaching the final where they were due to meet Queens Park, Vale of Leven were the side defaulting, after claiming that they were unable to find enough players to field a side.

62. SECOND COMING

Swiss Super League club FC Aarau experienced the second coming of Christ when, in February 1999, they re-signed 25-year-old midfielder Sven Christ, who they had sold to Grasshopper of Zurich some seasons earlier.

63. DOGGED BY BAD LUCK

Lincoln City were the first side automatically relegated from the Football League to the Conference, courtesy of a dog.

The canine, a police dog called Bryn, had bitten Torquay's Jim McNichol as he went to get the ball for a last-minute throw-in – and during the four minutes added on in the 1986-87 match, Torquay scored the equaliser against Crewe, which saved them from relegation, but sent City down.

64. NOW, LOOK – YOU'RE OFF

Burnley and England winger Billy Elliott may be the only player ever sent off for 'a threatening look' at an opponent.

Recalling the incident later, in 1999, the then 74-year-old commented, 'I only looked threatening without my top set of dentures.'

Those that saw him play say he was one of the hardest of the hard – as Burnley historian Dave Thomas commented: 'To be sent off in those days you really did have to commit something akin to murder. He was the only Burnley player sent off in a 20-year period. Burnley folk talked about it for weeks.'

Elliott, who had joined Burnley for a hefty £23,000 from Bradford in 1951, went on to become manager of Libya from 1961-63. He died in January 2008.

65. ISN'T THAT – OH, WHAT'S HIS NAME?

Hitler, as most football trivia addicts are aware, only ever attended one football match – the 1936 Germany versus Norway game in 1936, which they lost 2-0, causing him to leave the stadium before the end of the game.

However, author and historian of German football, Ulrich Hesse-Lichtenberger, believes Hitler might well also have been a spectator at a 1941 championship-deciding game between Schalke and Rapid Vienna, which featured a match-winning five-minute hat-trick by Rapid's Binder, citing 'reports that Hitler watched the game from the stands'.

66. BOOT MONEY

'Boot money' they called it – the cash stuffed into the boot in the days when it wasn't done to pay players openly, or when their wages were limited by a maximum wage.

But one of the first 'superstar' players to earn himself a little, literal boot money, by endorsing a brand of football boot was Blackburn Rovers star, Hugh McIntyre, who played for them from 1879-1886. McIntyre swore by – doubtless for a small fee – the Premier Boot manufactured by Mercer & Co of Bolton, who claimed to be the, ahem, 'sole' manufacturers of said footwear.

And what a slogan they came up with: 'Splendidly made and look good enough to play football themselves without any assistance.' Eat your hearts out Adidas, Nike and co.

67. ITALY'S BEST?

'The way he played was anarchic, and poetic. He scored beautiful, impossible goals and his spindly legs drove defenders to distraction.' It could have been George Best that Italian football historian John Foot was describing. But, no, it was a close Italian equivalent – the comparison extending to a focus on his hair. He refused to cut his hair in order to play for his country. He was even banned for failing to attend a drugs test which caught out three of those who did take it.

Gigi Meroni was born in 1943 and was playing for Torino in 1964 – with his socks rolled down to his ankles – and was nicknamed, after their shirt colour – the 'purple butterfly'.

A flamboyant dresser, he designed his own clothes and wore large sunglasses. He had an affair with a young, married woman.

In tune with the changing times, Moreni was keen on artistic 'happenings' and once, in his hometown, Como, took a friend in his smart sports car to the main square, where the two of them put a lead on a chicken they had brought with them, and proceeded to walk around the square before, perhaps symbolically, taking it to the local lake and dressing it, not wholly successfully, in a swimsuit.

When Juventus had an offer accepted, fans took to the streets in protest and the deal was called off.

In October 1967, Gigi and his teammate and partner in chicken-crime, Fabrizio Poletti, were out celebrating a 4-2 victory over Sampdoria. It was evening time and they were about to cross the road to get to a bar. Disaster struck as they crossed. Gigi was hit on the left leg and thrown across the road where a car struck him, dragging him along the road. Poletti was also hit but only slightly injured. The two were rushed to hospital, but nothing could be done for Gigi.

The first car to strike him was driven by 19 year old student and fanatical Torino supporter, and season-ticket holder, Attilio Romero. He had a poster of Gigi on his wall at home. He had been at the game that afternoon, lived in the same road as Gigi and even looked like him. More than 20,000 attended Gigi Meroni's funeral.

Gigi was never forgotten. In 2000 Torino appointed a lifelong supporter, and spokesman for Fiat, as President. He was Attilio Romero. The appointment was not well received by all fans – Romero had cries of 'murderer' shouted at him.

Three years later the woman with whom Gigi had had an affair returned to Italy after 22 years away and promptly alleged that Romero had stopped the club tradition of annually sending a wreath to Gigi's grave on his birthday and that he had never contacted the Meroni family to apologise.

Gigi's name is still sung at games, he has a dedicated website – gigimeroni.it – and his photograph is still displayed near the spot where he died.

68. NOT QUITE THE TICKET

Eva Standmann, 42, was mugged near the Munich Stadium shortly before the Brazil versus Australia World Cup match in June 2006. Her ticket for the game was in her handbag, stolen in the attack.

Mrs Standmann's husband, Berndt, 43, attended the match and was staggered when a man arrived to sit in the seat which should have housed his wife. He duly alerted the security guards and an unnamed 34-year-old man was arrested.

69. SIXTY NINER

Born in 1969; 1.69 metres tall and weighing 69kg – three of the reasons given by Bixente Lizarazu to explain why he turned out wearing the number 69 on his Bayern Munich shirt during the 2005-06 season.

What other explanation could there be that wouldn't turn his own on its head, I wonder?

⋆ £4 million Parma striker Cristiano Lucarelli wore 99 in homage to the left-wing political group, Brigate Autonome Livornesi, formed in 1999.

70. FULLY DESERVED – NO KID-DING

German Sports Personality of the Year for 2007 was Ivan Klasnic, a German-born Croatian striker who had had an unremarkable 12 months on the pitch – playing just a handful of games for Werder Bremen.

However, the 27-year-old's incredible struggle just to play again had captured the nation's imagination.

In late 2005 he was diagnosed as needing a kidney transplant – but his body rejected the one donated by his mother, following the January 2006 operation. Nonetheless, Werder stood by the player, extending his contract, and he underwent a second transplant, this time receiving a kidney from his father.

He battled back to fitness and returned to training in July 2007, playing his comeback game at Energie Cottbus in November, lasting 64 minutes, wearing a protective belt, before being substituted to a standing ovation. Within four weeks he notched his first two comeback goals in a 5-2 win over Bayer Leverkusen.

His experiences have made Klasnic philosophical: 'I have learned what is really important in life – that it is a beautiful day and that you can play football.'

71. FANS ACCUSED OF CASHING IN ON MUNICH DISASTER

Internet auction site eBay cracked down on the sale of commemorative Manchester United scarves which had been given away to fans attending the February 2008 local derby against Manchester City, marking the 50th anniversary of the Munich air disaster.

Hours after United's 1-2 defeat dozens of the scarves were being offered for sale on the site at up to £60 each before officials pulled the plug, saying 'the decision was taken in line with policy not to allow users to profit from human tragedy'.

72. MONK-EY BUSINESS

Former Chelsea star – well, player – Mateja Kezman announced in January 2008 that he wanted to become a monk when he retires. 'Serving the Lord is the greatest thing one can do. I visit monasteries whenever I can,' he declared, before confessing to one vice that probably wouldn't exclude him from his ambition: 'Tattoos are my only vice, but I am becoming less obsessed with them thanks to the Lord's help.'

Kezman's desire might confuse Sir Bobby Robson who once commented in his usual sage manner: 'Footballers can't be monks – we don't want them to be monks, we want them to be football players because a monk doesn't play football at this level.'

And Kezman might want to consider joining Romanian club Cetatea Targu Neamt, who in July 2007 informed players that they were going to train for ten days at a nearby monastery as they would benefit by training 'close to God'.

73. DOUBLE DUTCH

Former England manager Steve McLaren joined Dutch side, FC Twente, as boss in 2008 and became so immersed in the job that, bizarrely, he began speaking English with a cod Dutch accent.

A TV interview ahead of a Champions League clash with Arsenal recorded him telling an interviewer: 'Liverpool or Arsenal, I thought one of them we would draw … I say I think we are not just – what you call? – underdogs, but massive underdogs.'

He sounded for all the world like Martin Jol or Ruud Gullit, even down to the 'sh' sound of the letter 's', and lengthening of the 'v'.

Anyone else thinking it must make a change from the Double Dutch he spouted as England coach?

74. MARCO MY WORDS

It was perhaps the most shocking sending-off offence ever seen live on TV when France's universally admired Zinedine Zidane head-butted Italy's defender Marco Materazzi towards the end of the 2006 World Cup final, won by the Italians.

Precisely what was said to spark that sort of reaction from the normally imperturbable Zidane will probably never be known for sure, but one version has the Frenchman offering to swap shirts after the game only for the Italian to respond, 'I'd rather take the shirt off your wife.'

In another version Materazzi insulted Zidane's mother. Other sources claimed that Zidane had been called a 'dirty terrorist'.

Materazzi did not speak of the incident until August 2007 when he told *Sorrisi e Canzoni* magazine that Zidane had complained about the defender's tactics and told him: 'If you want my shirt that badly I'll give it to you after the game,' to which Materazzi had responded, 'I'd prefer your whore of a sister.'

Despite the sending off, Zidane still won the Golden Ball award for the best player at the tournament – although votes had been cast before the final.

In March 2008, Materazzi was given an apology and a 'substantial' payment from the *Daily Star* after the paper had wrongly accused him of racially abusing Zidane. The *Daily Star* had accused him of calling Zidane's mother a 'terrorist whore'. He also launched proceedings against other British newspapers, which had to issue apologies.

75. TRANSFERRING AFFECTIONS

Birmingham City managing director Karren Brady, who has won a Businesswoman of the Year award, took on the role at the Midlands club when she was just 23 – and was unique in the game in her role, which led to some interesting incidents when she went to away games and entered the previously male-dominated bastion of the boardroom at different clubs.

Within a year of joining Birmingham she met her future husband, one of their players, Paul Peschisolido. She sold him twice, but claims, 'It didn't affect our relationship. That's part of football – he understands what the process is. Every time we got short of cash he was always one of the assets that got sold off.'

Ms Brady once said of players: 'Most footballers are only really interested in drinking, clothes and the size of their willies.'

76. SPARTAK SPY

Despite having no top level experience of the game at home, Jim Riordan became the first English player to appear for Spartak Moscow (announced as Yakov Eeeordahnov), turning out for them in a central defensive role in two 1963 league matches, attended by up to 50,000 spectators.

Unbeknown to his team mates Riordan, living and working in Moscow, had been trained up as a spy during his National Service. He told the full story in his 2008 book *Comrade Jim*.

77. THE FERDINAND BLUES

Les Ferdinand, former Spurs, Newcastle and QPR striker, is frustrated that he is doomed forever to be associated with a story which appeared in The Sun claiming that he was responsible for an attack on the BBC's Blue Peter garden in Shepherds Bush, the part of London where he grew up.

He admits to joking about the incident during a BBC interview: 'They mentioned the Blue Peter garden and kept on mentioning it, so eventually, as a joke, I said that I might have helped someone over the wall.'

The Sun then ran a story claiming that Ferdinand had owned up to being the perpetrator of the incident – 'the problem is that when people see me now they don't think "That's Les Ferdinand, ex England international, but Les Ferdinand, the guy who wrecked the Blue Peter garden" – it drives me nuts.'

Ferdinand claims to have a letter from Blue Peter telling him that they know he had nothing to do with it, but knows he will always have the allegation hanging over him!

78. UNEXPECTED REWARD

Junior Agogo of Nottingham Forest is used to winning bonuses, but after he hit the goal that took his country Ghana into the semi-finals of the 2008 African Nations Cup, of which they were the host country, he was shocked when a fan offered him a most unusual reward for his goal.

The 82-year-old man, who gave his name as Nana, came to the team hotel in Accra where he told Agogo, according to newspaper reports: 'I came here last night with my very beautiful grand-daughter to introduce her: she is all yours.'

Agogo apparently told him, 'The fans show me so much love.'

79. JAMIE COULDN'T HAVE CAKE AND EAT IT

Jamie Carragher was given a splendid red cake to celebrate his 30th birthday in early 2008 – only for it to be stolen during the family party which was taking place at Liverpool's Sir Thomas Hotel.

But then a ransom note, together with a photograph of a slice of the missing, shirt-shaped cake was received, saying, 'We cut this bit off. If you want to see the rest, phone … the cake gets it unless our demands are met. Do not contact the cops.'

There were unconfirmed and frankly unlikely-sounding claims that the cake was stolen by fans belonging to a group called Sons of Shankly, as part of a protest against the club's American owners.

80. LONG AND THE SHORT OF IT...

Lincoln City's team during the 1958-59 season included the 6ft 3in defender Ray Long and the 5ft 2in striker Joe Short.

81. WE CAN LEG THIS LOT OVER

In a stunt designed to illustrate their capability of beating opponents Bolton on one leg, Manchester United employed a one-legged man to hop around wearing a red singlet and white shorts before the kick-off of the North Cup final at Maine Road in 1945. But after the match United didn't have a leg to stand on as Bolton beat them.

82. GETTING SHIRT SHRIFT

Umbro should be odds-on favourites to win the title for 'Worst Football Shirt Advertisement Ever' after inflicting on the public on the day of Fabio Capello's first game in charge of England, this monstrosity of copywriting catastrophe, designed to persuade people to part with some outrageous chunk of cash for a shirt much like the last one inflicted on them in the name of the national side:

'MORE THAN JUST A FOOTBALL SHIRT

BRING IT ON.' So read the ungrammatical, unpunctuated banner headline. But it got worse:

'THIS IS NOT JUST A FOOTBALL SHIRT. THIS IS A STATEMENT OF BELIEF.

DETERMINATION AND INTENT. THIS IS A DECLARATION OF SUPPORT AND PRIDE. THIS IS THE ENGLAND SHIRT.'

Sorry, people. This was NOT more than a football shirt. This was just that. A football shirt. And not a particularly appealingly designed one, at that. And this was just AN England shirt. Not THE England shirt. And they illustrated it with a photograph of Michael Owen wearing the shirt. The same Michael Owen who was dropped for Fabio's first game.

83. ERNIE'S PAYNE BOOTED SPURS INTO PROFESSIONALISM

The purchase of a pair of football boots was the catalyst to professionalism for Tottenham Hotspur.

When Ernest Payne left Fulham to join Spurs in 1893, he arrived at the then amateur club to discover that his kit was missing.

However, as he was joining a new club his old gear was obviously superfluous to requirements and he was duly given a set of socks, shorts and shirt in Spurs' colours, and the club gave him ten shillings (50p) with which to replace his lost boots.

When news of this arrangement somehow came to the ears of the London FA they promptly suspended Spurs for breaking the rules on amateurism. This was the final straw for the club, which had been contemplating joining the paid ranks, so they decided to set the wheels in motion for turning professional, which they duly achieved in 1895.

84. KEV'S RECORD ACHIEVEMENT

Kevin Keegan was the first superstar footballer to hit the record charts, when his *Head Over Heels In Love* charged into the Top 50 on June 9, 1979, staying there for six weeks and rising to the heady heights of number 31.

Kev never troubled the charts again, but in 1987 a duo called Glenn and Chris made a single called *Diamond Lights*, which struck a chord with the public and on April 18 arrived in the charts, making it to number 12 in an eight-week stay. They were Glenn Hoddle and Chris Waddle.

But, outdoing even this, and admittedly with the assistance of an established group, Lindisfarne, Paul Gascoigne, listed on the record label as 'Gazza', went to number two in the charts during a nine-week chart life for his *Fog On The Tyne (Revisited)* which entered in November 1990, and was followed up by his solo effort, *Geordie Boys (Gazza Rap)* which made number 31 in the Xmas chart of that year and stayed there for five weeks. Fortunately for the health of music in this country, that was his final stab at a musical career.

Interesting, how all three chart acts have a strong Geordie connection.

★ Tomas Brolin, who played in England for both Crystal Palace and Leeds, hit the Swedish top 20 in 1999 with *Alla Vi*, the video for which was banned for featuring 'too many breast implants and too few clothes'.

★ In 1971 *Good Old Arsenal* reached number 16 – with lyrics by Jimmy Hill.

★ Blackburn's winger, Morten Gamst Pedersen, fronted a boy-band, consisting of five Norwegian footballers, who released a charity single, *This Is For Real*.

85. GOOD VIBRATIONS

Chelsea star Michael Ballack and Bayern Munich's Oliver Kahn came in for a £34,000 windfall in May 2007 – after a German sex toy firm agreed to compensate the pair for using their names to sell vibrators.

Beate Uhse had been marketing the bright red, seven-inch long 'Michael B' and 'Olli K' devices, which retailed at £40 each, until the two stars found out and demanded recompense.

86. LEIGH'S CUNNING ROOSES

Leigh Richmond Roose was one of the most unconventional of goalkeepers – extraordinary, even among a galaxy of unorthodoxy in that position.

Born in 1878, he played for Stoke, Sunderland, Everton, Aston Villa and Arsenal as well as representing Wales before the First World War, from which he would never return.

His main superstition was a refusal to permit anyone to wash his shirt. 'Roose is one of the cleanest custodians we have, but is a trifle superstitious about his football garments, for he seldom seems to trouble the charwoman with them,' wrote the *Cricket & Football Field* magazine.

Once, during an international, Wales were reduced to ten men through injury, so Roose played at full back – while still keeping goal.

Before kick-off, Roose would pace from one side of his penalty area to the other, muttering to himself. He would often swing from the crossbar prior to games – unheard of in those days.

During quiet periods of play Roose would strike up conversations with members of the crowd, once conceding a goal against Scotland in that fashion in 1910.

The best part of a century before Bruce Grobbelaar, Roose was attempting to distract penalty takers by wobbling his knees and legs like a mad thing while awaiting the run-up.

He once turned up for a Wales game with his hand encased in bandages yet declared he would still play despite having a pair of broken fingers. He ran on to the pitch to find a crowd of photographers assembled to capture the unusual sight of a bandage-clad keeper, whereupon he unravelled the bandages and displayed his two entirely undamaged digits.

Before heading off to war, Roose declared, 'Before you go to war, say a prayer. Before going to sea, say two prayers. Before marrying, say three prayers. Before deciding to become a goalkeeper, say four prayers.'

Asked once by the Welsh FA in 1907-08 to justify an expenses claim – he demanded '4d for Pistol to ward off opposition. 3d; Coat and gloves to keep warm when not occupied' and '2d; Using the toilet (twice).'

Late for a Sunderland game once, he hired a locomotive to get him there on time – and billed the club.

He dated superstar of the music hall, Marie Lloyd.

He once upset Stoke supporters so much during a game by playing in goal against them wearing a Stoke shirt that they invaded the pitch and chased him to the nearby River Trent fully intending to cause him physical damage, from which he was eventually rescued.

Because of Roose's continuous – and entirely legal – exploitation of the rules of the day, which permitted keepers to carry the ball as far as the halfway line, although few did so, the rule was amended, forcing keepers to bounce, rather than carry the ball.

87. GAME OF TWO HALVES OR
HALVES OF TWO GAMES

Soren Lerby was substituted after 58 minutes of Denmark's November 1985 World Cup qualifying game in Dublin with the Danes in a comfortable 3-1 lead.

The left-footed midfielder barely had time to change before he was jumping into a private jet, organised by his German club side, Bayern Munich, and flown to Bochum, where he was brought on as a half-time substitute in a third round German Cup game in which he helped his side to a 1-1 draw.

88. AN ICE LITTLE EARNER

During the great freeze in the winter of 1963, Halifax Town were able to increase their income stream when they opened their ground up to the paying public as an ice rink.

89. PINK FLOYD – LEG-BREAKERS?

Rock drummer Chris Townson was perhaps one of the nearly-men of rock music – he was part of the legendary 1960s band, John's Children, whose front man, Marc Bolan, went on to greater glories with T Rex. Townson also played in bands like Jook, Jet and Radio Stars, all featuring top musicians, but for whom commercial success proved elusive. However, Townson does have one unique claim to fame – Pink Floyd were responsible for breaking his leg in a football match!

Townson revealed the story in a 2008 interview in specialist rock magazine, *Shindig*, explaining that he missed out on playing a series of live gigs with his band Jet, when 'I broke my leg playing football against Pink Floyd'. He elaborated: 'We first started playing football against them (Floyd) at rehearsal rooms in Fulham. It got quite nasty and we started having arguments. So I said to (Floyd bassist) Roger Waters, "You bring your team and I'll bring mine and we'll give you a proper football game". So he came to North London. I met them in Arnos Grove and got a pitch together and a team I played for and we played them on Sunday morning. And that's when I broke my leg.'

The score is not recorded. Sadly, Chris died in February 2008.

90. NAME?!

There were no reported bookings in the 1999 game between a team of former Mexican professionals, and a balaclava- and army boots-wearing Mexican guerrilla XI, representing the Zapatista National Liberation Army. The match, at the Jesus Martin Palillo Stadium, was played to gain publicity for their cause.

★ Roma lined up for a 1999 Serie A fixture against Cagliari wearing crash helmets to publicise a police motorbike safety drive.

91. YOU COULD SEE THROUGH THAT

Officials from the Isles of Scilly League announced a major sponsorship deal with an island-based double glazing company in December 1985. The news was received with delight by BOTH teams playing in the League – against each other – every week.

92. BARCA BOYCOTT

Barcelona refused to fly with German budget airline, Air Berlin – with which it had booked tickets to travel to America in August 2008 – when the airline declined a request to make in-flight announcements in the Catalan language of the region where Barcelona is based. Barca had to forfeit their costs as a result.

93. MARRIED TO THE CLUB

Japanese champions Kashima Antlers celebrated their tenth anniversary in 2001 by staging a series of fans' weddings at their stadium, at which a number of players gave celebratory readings.

But, we need to know – did the Antlers also host the stag nights?

94. NET RESULT

Writing on July 22, 2007, blogger '200percent' a knowledgeable observer of the football scene, wrote a history of goals and nets, during the course of which he issued an odd plea for help:

'I could swear that, on a visit to Parc Des Princes in about 1987, Paris St Germain had goal nets that lit up 'GOL!' in a crazy zig-zag shaped balloon when someone scored (since I can find no reference to it *anywhere*, I may have dreamt this – my memory tells me that they were discontinued after they started malfunctioning and flashing up 'GOL!' on any number of random occasions, but still I'm seeking some sort of confirmation on this from elsewhere, if anyone can provide any).'

If you can confirm or reject this memory, you'll find the blogger at 200percent. blogspot.com.

95. HAPPY-ISH BIRTHDAY, DEAR

Celebrating his 40th birthday in January 2006, an anonymous Manchester United fan wondered what his wife had bought him.

'Here you are dear,' she said, handing over the gift, which he opened up to discover was a current season ticket.

She had bought it at the start of the season, apparently not realising that it was valid for every game. The birthday blunder was revealed by a United fan sitting close to the man, who told reporters, 'We did wonder why the seat stayed empty for the first eleven games!'

96. ON YER BIKE, BOYS

Two Uzbekistan football fans were determined to get the autograph of their idol, German goalkeeper Oliver Kahn – so, in March 2006 they set off from Tashkent to cycle 4,000 miles across Europe.

Akram Marufshonow and Musadshon Chornidow's two-wheeled trek came to the attention of a German journalist who arranged for the pair to meet up with their hero in Berlin. When they were introduced to the World Cup keeper the pair burst into tears and hugged him, telling him 'You do not know what an honour this is for us' – in Uzbekistanish – Uzbekistani? – to which Khan responded, in German, 'I just can't believe this' and signed autographs for them.

97. SEVENTIES' LEGENDS – AS PRATS!

Who would believe that living legends like Kevin Keegan and Jimmy Greaves could have made complete and utter on-pitch prats of themselves.

Few now remember that on December 31, 1977, Keegan saw out the old year by being sent off after just six minutes of a friendly between his club of the time, Hamburg, and amateur side Lubeck, whose defender, Erhard Preuss, was left stretched out on the turf by a Keegan left-right combination after making a reckless tackle on the superstar. Kev was suspended for eight weeks, despite protestations that: 'All the frustration that had been building up over a difficult time trying to win acceptance at Hamburg erupted in one moment of wild anger. Trying to settle in Hamburg had been the closest I have been to hell, and only the love of my wife Jean kept me sane.'

Kev, get over yourself, mate.

Then, just ten days later one of England's finest ever strikers, Jimmy Greaves, who was playing out the final days of his career at then Southern League side Barnet, not only got himself sent off for swearing – he refused to leave the pitch and eventually forced the ref to abandon the match!

Afterwards, he still insisted he had never sworn, but was fined £25 and banned for four matches. Seventeen days later, Greaves was telling readers of the *Sunday People*: 'I've been warned that if I don't stop drinking I will slowly kill myself'.

And it wasn't only players losing it. England's most successful manager, Sir Alf Ramsey, found himself quitting as boss of Birmingham City in March, having become frustrated at a lack of support for his attitude to star striker, Trevor Francis. 'I wanted to put Francis on the transfer list but the board disagreed,' he complained. 'Francis has had his say in the newspapers, his wife has had her say – now I'm waiting for their dog to speak up. Some of today's overrated players don't want managers. They want nursemaids.'

Only a few months earlier, in July, Manchester United had dismissed boss Tommy Docherty – for having an affair with club physio's wife, Mary Brown. 'I have been punished for falling in love,' complained The Doc. Days after Ramsey quit, Docherty fell out of love – with Bruce Rioch, his player at current club, Derby. The former Scotland boss had a bust-up with the Scottish skipper – and suspended him for two weeks.

A day later everyone's favourite elder statesman of the game, Bobby Robson, then manager of Ipswich observed fans fighting during their Cup match against Millwall and commented: 'I would turn a flame-thrower on them.'

98. I'VE GOD TO GET OUT

Lincoln City fans were astonished when their manager Willie Bell announced in October 1978 that he was quitting his job so that he could 'find players for God'.

It transpired that Bell had joined an American-based religious sect and was to coach their football team, Crusade for Christ, which featured players who had been converted to Christianity.

99. FAIR ENOUGH, BUTT...

Having just been named FIFA Fair Player of 1996, Liberia's George Weah head-butted Porto player Jorge Costa while they were in the stadium tunnel as his club AC Milan were taking on Porto in a Champions League. It was a six-match-ban offence.

100. MORE IMPORTANT THAN LIFE ITSELF?

A Lazio fan killed himself after his favourite club sold star player Christian Vieri for a reported £30 million fee in June 1999; 25-year-old Elio Di Cristofalo threw himself under a train in Rome, and was decapitated.

His suicide note explained: 'I don't even know why I am still alive, Lazio have sold Vieri. All that money for a footballer, but money is not everything in life.'

101. DOGGED GREAVESIE WELL PIS*ED OFF

England were on their way out of the World Cup via a 3-1 defeat by Brazil in the 1962 tournament, but striker Jimmy Greaves was always one for a laugh on the pitch.

So, when a stray dog encroached on to the playing field and evaded attempts to catch him, Jimmy dropped down on all fours and barked and beckoned to the dog, eventually persuading him to come close enough to grab him.

When Greavesie did catch the dog, he suddenly wished he hadn't, as it urinated all over him. 'I smelt so bad it was awful – but at least the Brazilian defenders stayed clear of me.'

A Brazilian official apparently kept hold of the dog and after the match he gave it away in a free raffle for the squad – won by Garrincha, the star player known as the Little Bird, who reportedly then kept the animal, named Bi.

102. AND THEIR DEFENCE HAS GONE MISSING!

Chile received an easy ride to West Germany's World Cup of 1974 when the Soviet Union refused to play the South Americans in the second leg of a special qualifying play-off. After playing a scoreless draw in Moscow, the Soviets refused to play at Estadio Nacional in Santiago, claiming left-wing prisoners had been shot there. FIFA threw the Soviets out of the tournament.

To make their qualification official, the Chilean team lined up in Estadio Nacional against the 'phantom' Soviet team, dribbled down the field, and scored.

✳ In October 1996 Scotland kicked off in their away World Cup qualifier versus Estonia at the scheduled kick off time of 3pm. The game was abandoned after three seconds – as Estonia had not turned up because of a row over floodlights at the stadium. Estonia arrived and also kicked off alone at the originally scheduled 18.45 kick off time. The match was actually played in Monte Carlo, Scotland winning 2-0.

103. LACK OF TRAINING

Ready to catch the train to Leipzig for the 1903 German football championships, where they would take on German Bohemians of Prague in the semi-final, officials of South German champions, FV Karlsruhe, widely believed to be the best side left in the tournament, received a telegram stating: 'Match postponed. More news forthcoming.'

They duly stood the players down and sent them home to await further instructions. None arrived and their opponents were awarded the game because of this no-show.

'To this day, people in Karlsruhe are trying to find out who sent that false and fateful telegram,' said German football historian, Ulrich Hesse-Lichtenberger, suggesting that the Bohemians, who went through as a result were 'either lucky or cunning'.

They got their comeuppance, though, losing to VfB Leipzig in the final.

104. VILLAINS BY NAME

Rumours abounded that Aston Villa's pampered players were misbehaving away from the club, not getting into the right frame of mind to prepare for games, and letting themselves down by carousing with the wrong sort of people.

So, Villa's bosses decided on a drastic move to find out for sure what was going on. After all, Villa were among the title contenders. They hired a Birmingham private detective, and instructed him to keep an eye on their stars, to make sure they weren't adversely affecting their own and their club's reputation.

The 'tec reported back that a number of players had been drinking and partying to excess – and three of them, Cowan, Crabtree and Wheldon, were dropped for the next match.

And when was this monitoring of glamorous, highly paid superstars going on? During the 1899-1900 season! It obviously had the desired effect as Aston Villa went on to clinch the title.

105. NOT BIKELY

Chelsea stewards have been instructed since March 2007 to prevent fans from smuggling sticks of celery into the ground, which have been known to be waved around as part of some bizarre Stamford Bridge chant, believed to contain the following verse: 'Celery, celery; If she don't come; I'll tickle her bum. With a lump of celery.'

Stewards at Inter Milan have had to be on their guard against rather more heavy duty smuggling since an incident during 2002, which saw their hard core, 'curva' fans somehow manage to smuggle a motorbike into the second tier of the stadium when there was a game against Atalanta – from which area the motorbike's licence plate emanated – going on.

Once the vehicle had emerged, a group of fans promptly battered it to within an inch of its motorised life before pushing it over the edge of the barrier and seeing it crash to the – fortunately empty – terraces underneath.

106. FLUSHING HIS CAREER DOWN THE TOILET

Former Chelsea full-back Glen Johnson, who joined Portsmouth, was given an on the spot fine of £80 by Kent police after being accused of deliberately switching an expensive toilet seat into the box of a cheaper variety, which he then endeavoured to 'smuggle' through the check-out of a B&Q store in Dartford in January 2007.

107. STRICTLY FOR THE BIRDS

Gremio of Brazil earned a point in their October 2002 game against Botafogo when striker Fabio's goal-bound shot was deflected away from their net by a giant Lapwing which swooped down on the pitch at just that moment.

'Unfortunately, the bird was not injured,' moaned Botafogo's Ademilson, and Gremio fans chanted 'Quero, quero' ('Lapwing, lapwing').

✱ Danny Worthington's high cross into the Hollingworth box found its way into the net when the effort by the Greater Manchester-based Stalybridge Celtic Colts' 13-year-old made contact with the beak of a passing seagull. The FA's Steve Double declared it a first: 'To the best of my knowledge, a seagull has never scored before.'

108. PIGGING OUT

Play stopped for 20 minutes in a 2004 Austrian Cup quarter-final between Watten Wacker and SV Salzburg as stewards tried to catch Hans, a piglet.

⋆ Worthing player Dave Clark faced a disciplinary hearing after nailing a pig's head to the dugout of rivals Eastbourne in February 1997.

109. WORD IN YOUR EAR, MATE

Richard Hofmann, star of the German national side, played with a bandage over his head, having lost his right ear in a car accident two months before a game with England in May 1930.

The papers dubbed him – in German, of course – 'King Richard the Lionheart.'

In 1933 Hofmann was kicked out of the national side for accepting 3,000 marks for posing for a cigarette advertisement. He was a non-smoker.

110. HORSING ABOUT

Striker Geoff Horsfield was not entirely flattered in August 1999 when Fulham fans sponsored an animal at London Zoo in his 'honour' – a tortoise.

Horsfield is one of several players who have been associated with a popular terrace chant – 'Feed the horse and he will score'. Others include Sean Goater – 'Feed the goat and he will score' and Everton's Yakubu Aiyegbeni – 'Feed the yak and he will score'.

111. THAT SANDY

When Sunderland centre-half and Scottish international Sandy McAllister finally scored his first goal for the club on his 111th appearance at Preston on January 5, 1901, earning them a draw, supporters were so delighted that they clubbed together to buy him a piano – and a gold watch.

112. IN PRIME POSITION

Prime Minister Gordon Brown, a Raith Rovers supporter, has made half-hearted efforts to convince the electorate that he supports England during big tournaments if his own country is out. His predecessor Tony Blair delighted in stories of how devoted a Newcastle fan he is, despite suggestions that some of the players he claimed to have watched as a boy had actually left the club before he was born!

But the late Harold Wilson, another Labour Prime Minister, was definitely a confirmed and loyal Huddersfield Town supporter – with the bruises to prove it.

Lord Wilson, as he was by then, recalled in 1984 how he had attended the April 1926 Huddersfield v West Ham match as a young boy – 'and it provided me with my proudest moment in football'.

Wilson had parked himself on the terraces near one of the corner flags. He recalled how many years later he had met Town winger Alec Jackson and discussed that game in which, as Jackson remembered, he had come back to help with defensive duties late on, kicking the ball out for a corner and in the process seeing it hit a young lad in the face.

'I know.' Wilson told Jackson. 'That little boy was me. It was the proudest moment of my football life – being knocked over by a shot from the immortal Alec Jackson!'

113. ULTIMATE REACTION

Syd King, manager of West Ham since 1902, and under whom they reached the first ever Wembley Cup Final, was sacked in contentious circumstances involving allegations of drunkenness and financial irregularities on November 7, 1932.

Within a month of the sacking, King committed suicide 'by consuming an alcoholic beverage laced with a corrosive liquid' according to Kirk Blows' and Tony Hogg's *Essential History* of the club.

114. REFS ARE NO FOOLS

Football League officials showed all too rare evidence of a sense of humour when deciding which combinations of referee and linesmen to allocate for games on April 1, 2000.

Clubs thought they were being 'fooled' when they saw who was taking charge of their matches: Messrs Barber, Bone and Head were allocated to Luton's home game against Colchester, while Conn and Merchant teamed up at Southend and Coffey and Kettle arrived at Crewe.

Bannister and Hall officiated at Blackpool; North and West took charge at Bristol Rovers. Styles, Downs and Hills were the squad at Wycombe; Castle, Knight and King were at Mansfield; with Francis and Lee handed Gillingham.

Perhaps, though, the *piece de resistance* was at Peterborough, where the game was handled by Messrs Lynch, Deadman and Payne.

115. THAT'S DUNG IT

The Caernarfon League match between Llanrug United and Waunfawr was called off in November 1999, when referee Mike Griffiths ruled that the amount of sheep dung deposited on the playing surface represented a health risk.

116. THANK GOD FOR THAT

Lee Bradbury had failed to score for 12 games for his side Portsmouth. So, before he ran out to play Swindon in March 2000, he asked the club chaplain, the Rev Graham Carey, to say a prayer for him. Bradbury scored a hat-trick in the 4-1 win.

117. FENGS AIN'T WHAT THEY USED TO BE

When a TV company contacted Bristol Rovers offering to bring in experts in Feng Shui to improve the club's performances they allowed the two, Guy de Beaujeu and Patrick Stockhausen, to implement bizarre 'improvements' such as installing a fish tank behind a goal, putting a ceramic frog above the main gate, ensuring that lavatory seats in the ground were always down and hanging wind chimes around the ground. Rovers lost their next game against Gillingham in January 2000 by 1-0.

It was then revealed that the Feng Shui 'experts' were actually hoaxers from a programme called *Gatecrashers*.

118. HERE IS THE NUDES

Paulo Mata, coach of Brazilian side Itaperuna, raced on to the pitch, dropped his trousers, and mooned at the referee who had just awarded a controversial goal to condemn his side to a 3-2 defeat in 1997: 'I went naked because I'm tired of working honestly, only to be scandalously robbed,' he claimed.

★ Scunthorpe manager Brian Laws stripped striker Steve Guinan virtually naked in the club car park after the player declined to extend his loan from Nottingham Forest in November 1999. Laws demanded the instant return of Guinan's club tracksuit, leaving him half naked and shivering. 'I only want players who want to play for Scunthorpe wearing our tracksuits,' he explained.

* Brazilian international Vampeta posed naked in gay publication *G Magazine* in 1998. 'I'm doing it for the money,' he said.

* Norwegian club Rosenborg banned female journalists from their changing rooms in 1999 – 'I'm married, and the only woman allowed to see me naked is my wife,' said skipper Jahn Ivar Jakobsen, covering his modesty, to which reporter Mari By Rise of the *Dagbladet* newspaper responded: 'When I'm working I have neither the time nor the desire to study what the boys look like without clothes.'

* German club Preussen Frankfurt's boss Guenter Draieger came up with a unique incentive for his side in early 2000. A national newspaper reported that he had introduced what he called 'a new kind of warm-up' which involved 'pepping up the players by tying them to chairs and allowing a stripper to perform just inches away'.

* All of the Premiership matches on the final day of the 1996-97 season were livened up by pitch invasions from topless girls – thanks to lads' mag *Loaded*.

119. REF PEGS OUT

Swedish ref Timo Hietala astonished Arsenal and England striker Ian Wright – by attaching 84 clothes pegs to his face.

It happened in July 1999 when Hietala set a new world record, recognised by Guinness, for the greatest number of clothes pegs attached to a human face.

Wright was presenting the TV show on which the record bid was achieved, and seemed delighted to see a referee in pain.

120. FIVE BOOKINGS AND A SENDING OFF

Brighton Dockers FC of the Sussex Sunday League found it difficult during season 1997-98 to control one of their representatives, who received five bookings and a sending off.

Tina Gravett owned up to the offences – administered to her despite the fact that she was only a spectator at their matches.

'I can't help myself,' confessed the 42-year-old, 'I just want to show my support.'

121. WOMANSFIELD?

Mansfield Town Ladies Football Club landed a 1998 shirt sponsorship deal with a local brewery – whose motto was 'Man's World; Man's Pint; Mansfield'.

122. DIVINE INTERVENTION

Adriano Basso, Bristol City's Brazilian keeper, knew who to thank when he saved Watford striker Darius Henderson's penalty in March 2008: 'I always ask the Holy Spirit where they're going to kick it. He said "left" and I said "thank you". I went to the left side and I saved the ball. I was blessed.'

123. LACK OF MORAL COURAGE

The temptations available to superstar footballers of the 21st century are well chronicled – but those that threatened to lure their 19th century counterparts off the straight and narrow, less so.

In the official Tottenham Hotspurs handbook for season 1899-1900, readers were told: 'The team's successes in Cup ties were appreciated by the public in a way that was, to put it mildly, detrimental to the players, who were encouraged to excess in every direction.

'Some of the men had not the moral courage to resist this mistaken kindness, and as a result they have had to seek pastures anew.'

Not a bad excuse for shipping out the surplus Spurs, I suppose.

124. GOING ONE BETTER

Psychiatrist and referee Dr John Gayford booked all 22 players during a 1991 reserve game between Croydon Municipal Officers and Merton Officers. 'Dr Gayford should get help,' said Croydon secretary Tony Osborn.

In the same season, the referee in a Spanish match between Toledo Imperial and Gamonal took it so badly when he was 'insulted gravely' that he sent every player off.

125. WELL KITTED OUT

Helen Perschky applied for the job of kit manager for Conference side Stevenage during the 1998-99 season. The 25-year-old mum was delighted to be told she'd got the job – only to receive a follow-up phone call from the club the next day, telling her that club boss Richard Hill had vetoed her appointment 'because she was too attractive, and could distract the players'.

126. SORRY, CHAPS, WE WERE TOO BUSY

Rossendale United officials were devastated to discover that their clubhouse had suffered damage and theft during a break-in – but they were gobsmacked when it transpired that the culprits had offered to hand themselves in to the law, only to be told that the police were too busy to deal with them.

Serial thief and heroin addict Liam Tomlinson, 21, and another man broke into the clubhouse at Newchurch, near Rawtenstall, Lancashire in December 2007. The pair drank three bottles of spirits and then rang to tell police that they wanted to give themselves up, telling officers where they were. However, police were dealing with another incident and said they had no officers available.

When they finally reached the location the burglars had told them they would be, they discovered that they had grown tired of waiting and caused £2,500 of damage.

Tomlinson was eventually caught and given an eight-month prison sentence in February 2008 after admitting burglary, but his accomplice had not been traced. Inspector Dave Hodson said that officers had been alerted by an alarm at the clubhouse but found no-one there when they arrived and were busy elsewhere when the culprits phoned them.

127. LION-HEARTED PLAYER

Aston Villa sold Scottish international Robert (Bobby) Templeton for £400 in 1903. His new employers, Newcastle, wondered just what sort of player they had acquired when the players enjoyed a night at the local circus, and Templeton won a bet from one of his teammates by placing his head in a lion's mouth.

The fiery left-winger left the Toon shortly after he picked – and lost – a dressing-room fight with Albert Gosnall, who had replaced Templeton in the side when he was out injured.

128. I'M OUT OF HERE

When 31-year-old Arminia Bielefeld keeper Goran Curko slipped and almost conceded an own goal during an October 2000 German 2nd Division match with Waldhof Mannheim, his own fans turned on him and chanted 'Curko out'.

So, Curko went.

To the astonishment of the crowd, Curko just walked off, acquiring a yellow card on the way from a bemused referee.

Refusing to come back, Curko was replaced by young sub Dennis Eilhoff, who made an unexpected debut, keeping a clean sheet in the process.

The closest Curko came to an explanation was to say: 'I was simply not able to continue playing.'

129. BRANDI'S SPIRITED STRIP

After scoring the winning goal in the 1999 Women's World Cup final penalty shoot-out against China, the USA's Brandi Chastain promptly stripped off her shirt – revealing a black sports bra. She later said her impromptu strip was 'momentary insanity, nothing more, nothing less'.

Previously, Chastain had courted controversy by appearing nude, but for a strategically placed football, in glossy magazine Gear, justifying it by declaring: 'Hey, I ran my ass off for this body.'

Still, with her skipper, Julie Foudy, describing herself and her teammates as 'Booters with hooters', perhaps it wasn't entirely astounding that Chastain should explain her team's philosophy by saying, 'We're women who like to knock people's heads off and then put on a skirt and go dance.'

Brandi went on to write a book called *It's Not About the Bra*.

130. FA DIDN'T HAVE A LEG TO STAND ON

Leicestershire lad Sam Burrows, 12, was delighted to be picked for Lutterworth Town's youth side – but then devastated to be banned from playing for having a false leg.

His dad, Alan, launched a three-month battle to persuade the FA to make an exception from its own rule saying that players must not wear anything that could injure themselves or others.

Sam was finally allowed to turn out in a November 1998 game for his team, making him the first disabled player to appear in a competition recognised by the FA. They lost 6-1 but Sam didn't care.

131. TROLLEY GOOD?

After setting off at 5am from his Helsinki home to watch his favourite team, Torquay, play Chester in a February 2000 3rd Division game, 45-year-old Graham Tanner missed the entire first half when his train was held up between Nuneaton and Stafford – by a shopping trolley on the line.

Probably the wrong sort of shopping trolley, too.

When he finally arrived, it was to see Torquay lose 2-1.

132. GRAVE DELAY

Games involving German club MSV Duisburg in the early part of the 20th century were subject to unusual delays.

The club played on a ground next to a cemetery and the referee was frequently forced to call a halt to proceedings on the pitch while undertakers carried coffins across the ground, closely followed by the mourners.

133. THE RESULT IS A THAI

Thai footballer Samang Suwansri, 29, set a new world record in May 2000 by keeping a football airborne for 15 hours, while performing Thai dances, and eating noodles.

When calls of nature came, Samang balanced the ball on his head and entered a specially constructed toilet with waist high walls, enabling the judges to see that the ball had not touched the floor of the Bangkok department store in which he set the record.

134. TEAM FULL OF STRIKERS

England players threatened to go on strike before their 1909 international against Scotland.

The Players Union had only recently been formed, and was affiliated to the General Federation of Trades Unions, at a time when a wide-scale general strike was on the cards. The FA warned players that in the event of a general strike they must not join in.

The players considered a collective refusal to play the match, but eventually backed down and signed a statement issued on their behalf, which declared: 'Notwithstanding what has appeared in the Press, there was never the slightest doubt as to our determination to play our hardest and to do our best to accomplish a victory for England.'

Mmm.

England won 3-0.

135. WHISTLE FOR IT

Dutch ref Leo Horn took exception when Real Madrid's star forward, Puskas, argued over a decision that went against him during the 1962 European Cup final between his side and Benfica, who went on to win 5-3.

Horn threw his gold-plated whistle at the Hungarian. 'A good shot – right in the ear,' he later remembered.

* When France were awarded a goal from a quickly taken free-kick against Kuwait in the 1982 World Cup, Kuwaiti FA president Prince Fahid stormed on to the pitch, protesting that a whistle from the crowd had caused his side to stop playing. He threatened to take his team, losing 3-1, off the pitch. Referee Miroslav Stupar reversed his decision, the game continued – and France scored again.

* Striker Lee Todd was taken by surprise when the ref blew to start his game for Cross Farm Celtic in October 2000. Standing right in front of the ref, the blast on the whistle temporarily deafened him and he swore, 'F*** me, that was loud!' He was sent off – two seconds into the game – and fined £27. His team still beat Taunton East Reach Rovers 11-2.

136. FOOTBALL'S KILLER DOLPHIN

A Dutch woman was killed by a football-playing dolphin in July 1996.

The 64-year-old victim was visiting a fun park in Harderwijk, Holland and watched as the dolphin balanced a football on his nose and then flipped it into the crowd. It headed in her direction, then hit her on the head, causing her to slip and fall to her death down a flight of steps.

137. UPSON'S DOWN

West Ham defender Matthew Upson splashed out on a £100,000 Lamborghini – only to discover when it was delivered that his 6ft 1in frame was too bulky to get into the driver's seat.

So, with less than 400 miles on the clock, the 28-year-old had to sell the car – at a considerable loss.

'I couldn't fit into it,' he confessed in April 2008, 'I only did about 400 miles in it before I had to sell it – it was killing my back.'

138. TAXI, TAXI, TAXI, TAXI, TAXI, TAXI, TAXI ...

One hundred Sunderland supporters were left stranded after a Championship game at Cardiff in April 2007, which they had won 1-0.

The fans were at Bristol airport waiting to fly back but after easyJet stewards evicted a number of supporters they claimed were being unruly their scheduled flight missed its take-off slot and was axed.

Among those on board was Sunderland chairman Niall Quinn, who not only defended his fans against the easyJet allegations – 'A few had been drinking, but it was very good-natured' – but then announced that he would arrange taxis to take the fans home, at a personal cost to him of £8,000.

He hired 18 cabs to take them on the 300-mile journey back home – travelling in one himself. 'Thankfully everyone returned home safely,' he said, 'To any fans who still feel aggrieved, remember the three points came home as well.'

EasyJet commented: 'We have zero tolerance towards unacceptable behaviour.'

139. PIE-EYED

Most football fans have heard that Fatty Foulkes was a 24-stone goalkeeper before the First World War, who played for Chelsea and Sheffield United.

Fewer are aware that, in the years before his death in 1916, he toured the fairgrounds of the country, charging cash to all-comers to take him on in prize penalty competitions.

Fatty – real name Willie – was so huge that an opponent once suggested that the outline of an average-sized keeper should be etched on to him, and that if the ball hit outside that line a goal should be awarded.

However, it has only recently emerged that Foulkes was the inspiration for a terrace chant still in use to this day: 'Who ate all the pies?' sung to the tune of the old party piece, *Knees Up Mother Brown*.

Researchers for *The Penguin Book of Cliches* discovered that the song was originally aimed at Foulkes in 1894 – by his own fans.

Whether they also originated the refrain 'You fat bas*ard, you fat bas*ard, you ate all the pies!' is doubtful.

The same researchers also declared that another football favourite, 'I'm over the moon' comes, appropriately enough, from the nursery rhyme, 'the cow jumped over the moon' and was first purloined by Victorian aristocrats as part of their upmarket slang.

140. THE BANNER GOES – OR I DO!

The French president, Nicolas Sarkozy, attended the French League Cup final between Paris St-Germain and northern French club Racing Club de Lens in March 2008 – but he threatened to walk out at the start of the second half.

Sarkozy had taken one look at the 30-metre long banner which had been smuggled into the stadium in squares of cloth and then assembled and strung along the front of a stand, declaring 'Pedophiles, chomeurs, consanguins: bienvenue chez les ch'tis' – and demanded that it be torn down or he would walk out.

The banner, made by Paris fans, translated into: 'Paedophiles, unemployed and in-breds: welcome to the home of the ch'tis'.

Ch'tis are natives of the most northerly French region, the Nord-Pas de Calais.

After Sarkozy's threat was made to French Football League president Frederic Thiriez, the banner was removed within four minutes.

But it sparked a row after the game, won 2-1 by PSG, when politicians called for the game to be replayed.

Sarkozy's spokesman said he had been a 'shocked witness of the display of a hate-mongering banner'.

141. DREAM ON, MAN

Mansfield Town were the subject of a takeover bid by businessman John Batchelor in March 2008.

But Batchelor's bid for the struggling League Two side caused fans of the club some concern when he revealed that if he was successful he intended to change the club's name – to Harchester United – the name of the fictitious club featured in the SkyTV soccer soap opera, *Dream Team*.

And Batchelor – who previously owned York City, where he changed their name to York City Soccer Club in a bid to attract US tourists to their games – was also planning to involve actors from that programme in pre-season friendlies to boost crowds.

Batchelor was determined to push his idea through even against objections from the Football League: 'There is an easy solution – get relegated (into the Conference), then get promoted.'

At the same time, Accrington Stanley announced that they were seriously considering changing their name to Lancashire Stanley. The idea had begun as an April Fool's joke which had received a positive response.

142. WHITE CHRISTMAS

Bradford City had 20,000 Christmas cards printed in 1999, featuring their squad line-up. However, when star player Darren Moore left, they decided to replace him with new boy Neil Redfearn, by superimposing the face of the new arrival on to the body of the departing Moore.

Brilliant idea – up to a point. Moore is black. Redfearn white.

143. A RIGHT CHARLIE

For no better reason than that I believe him to have the greatest name ever given to a footballer, you should be aware of the career of the versatile forward who played at inside left, inside right and centre forward during a career that took him to Clapton Orient where he played 101 games, scoring 24 times, from 1921-24; then on to Manchester United from 1924-26 for 60 games and 24 goals before joining, but never playing for, Grimsby and Accrington Stanley.

Take a bow, Clatworthy Rennox – known to teammates as Charlie.

144. MOLDY OLD BET

Comedians Arthur Smith and Tony Hawks struck a bizarre bet when the former challenged the latter to find and beat at tennis every member of the Moldovan national team that had just been beaten by England in a World Cup qualifying game.

Hawks accepted the bet, flying to Moldova where he tracked down seven members of the side, managing to play and beat all of them. He then mopped up the remaining members of the squad when they flew to Belfast for a game against Northern Ireland.

Then, in early 1999, he met up with Smith in the Bedford Arms Pub in Balham High Street, London and the latter settled his losses – by stripping off and running down the road while singing the Moldovan national anthem.

145. DIRTY MONEY

Taking umbrage at a *Birmingham Gazette* report of their match at WBA in October 1893, Newton Heath sued the paper, which had accused them of dirty play.

The jury found in their favour – but awarded them just one farthing in damages.

146. BEATEN? NOT US!

The defeat of hot favourites the Soviet Union, by Yugoslavia in the second round of the 1952 Olympics football tournament was such an upset that neither the match nor its result was referred to by the Soviet media until after the death of Stalin a year later.

147. RACING, RINK – WRECKED

Hamilton Academicals decided to console themselves after being relegated to Scottish Division 3 in season 2000-2001. The players organised a trip to the local racecourse, and they then went on to the local ice rink where centre-back Ross MacLaren became the centre of attention when he waltzed around the rink with his underpants on his head and very few clothes adorning the rest of his body.

After the local constabulary had been invited along to enjoy the view of the naked reveller, MacLaren commented: 'It's been such a disappointing end to the season, so I thought I'd do something to cheer the guys up.'

148. EXTRA, EXTRA, EXTRA TIME

Playing a replay in the 1946 Third Division North Cup, after Stockport County and Doncaster had drawn 2-2 in the first game at Belle Vue, the two sides were still level after extra-time in the second game.

The teams were asked to play on to get a result.

Eighty-three minutes later neither side had been able to break the deadlock, so the game was abandoned due to bad light.

149. MARSVELLOUS

Dave Beasant recalled playing for Wimbledon in the old Fourth Division, against Hartlepool, when a Mars bar was thrown at him during the game.

'It missed, landing just beside me. I picked it up, gestured my thanks to the fans behind the goal and carried on.

'A short time later I was on the edge of my penalty box when there was an outbreak of cheering. I looked round and saw a young boy in the back of the goal net, looking through my glove bag to reclaim his Mars bar. When he found it he held it up like a trophy, and leapt back over the barrier into the crowd.'

150. NUTS ABOUT BRAZILIAN MEMORABILIA

One hundred and fifty copies of a 'Carnival' edition of Pele's official autobiography were produced by publishing house Gloria, who secured the rights to the project in 2005.

To make the books truly unique they decided to include with each £4,000 copy a print of the 1970 World Cup-winning Brazil team – signed by the coach, Zagallo, and each of the surviving players. Everaldo was the first, and at the time of going to press, only, one to have died.

The publisher planned to pay each player $1,000 to sign each of the 150 prints. (So, $1,000 per player for 150 signatures = approx £3.50 per signature, plus cost of print – not a bad mark-up for the publishers, one might think, as the 'Samba' copy of the book WITHOUT the print cost £2,000!)

All the players eventually went along with the plan, although Jairzinho initially held out for $10,000, later settling for $2,000, as did Rivelino. Tostao insisted that his fee, plus a pro-rata donation for profits from the use of his name, be donated to five Brazilian charities.

Gerson refused to sign until the publisher agreed to print a small, illustrated book on the charity he was running for underprivileged children.

The Carnival edition sold out quickly and now sells for much more than the original price, but the Samba edition, signed only by Pele, is still available at £2,000, details from www.number10shirt.com.

These are the players who beat Italy in the 1970 World Cup: Felix; Carlos Alberto; Brito; Jairzinho; Tostao; Gerson; Piazza; Rivelino; Clodoaldo; Pele; Everaldo.

151. CZECHING OUT

An odd story involving Czechs concerns the 1920 Olympic final in which Czechoslovakia were playing Belgium, who went two goals up through a tenth-minute disputed penalty and a 28th minute second which the Czechs were adamant was offside.

Both these goals were awarded by 72-year-old ref John Lewis, an Englishman who had officiated at a very controversial 4-0 win by England over Bohemia in Prague in 1908 when another disputed penalty had set up the victory, after which he had been assaulted by Bohemian fans.

The Czechs felt he was against them and when he then sent off a Czech player, Steiner, their whole team walked off – and would not return, eventually forfeiting the game. It is still the only abandoned international final in the game's history.

152. SPLIT PERSONALITY

Hadjuk Split defender Goran Granic announced in November 2005 that he had found God and therefore could no longer commit fouls.

The Croatian had been criticised after abandoning his trademark tough tackles, but explained to his local paper, *Slobodna Dalmacija*: 'I'm so devoted to God now that I have started to avoid committing fouls during matches. God has created football for fun and relaxation. He would not like players to commit harsh fouls.'

153. COUPLE OF WINKERS?

Cristiano Ronaldo was pilloried by the British media for winking during the 2006 World Cup.

The Manchester United winger did it while playing for his country Portugal in their win over England, during which his United teammate Wayne Rooney was red-carded, many believed after being wound up by Ronaldo, who then winked towards his bench.

At one point Ronaldo's future at United was believed to have been so compromised by that flick of an eyelid that my company, William Hill, offered 6-1 that he would still be at Old Trafford when the next season kicked off.

Referee Graham Poll must have sympathised with Ronaldo's plight when he, too, became a target for abuse during the same tournament after he made one of the most humiliating public refereeing blunders ever seen.

Reffing the Australia v Croatia game, Poll yellow-carded a Croatian player twice without sending him off – and only did so when he flourished a third yellow to the same player, leading *The Sun* to run the headline, 'Poll's Three Card Thick'.

154. WHEN PUSKAS CAME TO SHOVE

All serious football fans are aware that the 1960 European Cup final between Real Madrid and Eintracht Frankfurt, which ended 7-3 to the Spanish side, is one of the greatest club matches.

Few, though, remember now that the game very nearly did not take place.

Real star Ferenc Puskas had, shortly after the 1954 World Cup final in which his Hungary side, the hot favourites, had lost to West Germany, accused the winners of being doped to win.

The German football authority, the DFB, took extreme umbrage at this slur – and banned its clubs from taking part in matches against clubs for which Puskas was playing.

It took a great deal of behind-the-scenes diplomacy to prevent the European Cup final from being a non-event, with only one side turning up.

After Puskas had been 'persuaded' to write a formal letter of apology, the DFB were given a convenient get-out which did not make them look as though they had had to make an embarrassing climb-down, and the game was played.

155. SOCKET TO ME

David Bentley, of England and Spurs, has an odd obsession – plug sockets.

'I have to turn them off everywhere I go. At the training ground, in hotels, at away games,' he told *Observer Sports Monthly* in April 2008.

'I can't stand how the cleaners leave them on. I have to remind myself, walk away from the plug socket.'

156. OVER-EGGING THE PUDDING?

Two major celebrities have produced slightly baffling egg-related quotes about football.

Eccentric pop star Bjork observed in 2008: 'Football is a fertility festival. Eleven sperm trying to get into the egg. I feel sorry for the goalkeeper.'

Jose Mourinho was quoted in September 2007 as saying about the game: 'It's all about omelettes and eggs. No eggs, no omelette. And it depends on the quality of the eggs. In the supermarket, you have eggs class one, class two, class three. Some are more expensive than others, and some give you better omelettes. So when the class one eggs are in Waitrose and you cannot go there you have a problem.'

Eggs-actly, Jose. Aidan Davison, in goal for Grimsby during their 1998 Second Division play-off game at Fulham might have sympathised – after being felled by a hard-boiled egg hurled from the crowd.

157. NOT SO GLAD CHARLIE

Devastated after conceding the own goal that gave Newcastle a draw in their March 1913 FA Cup quarter-final replay against his side Sunderland, defender Charlie Gladwin was making his way home on a tramcar after the match when a fellow passenger, evidently unaware that Gladwin was on the vehicle, said to his companion, 'I wonder how much Gladwin got for putting the ball through his own goal.'

Gladwin approached the passenger and thumped him on the chin, knocking him off the vehicle and on to his back on the road.

170. WHAT WOULD CASTRO HAVE THOUGHT?

Cuba found themselves reduced to ten men as they lined up to play Honduras in a 2008 Olympic qualifying match.

They were competing in a round-robin qualification tournament in Florida, and after drawing their first game against USA 1-1, seven of their squad, including skipper Yenier Bermudez, vanished, believed to have defected, prompting Cuban FA official Antonio Garces to condemn the players – 'This was an irresponsible act of cowardice'.

Cuba duly lost 2-0 to Honduras.

171. FITNESS DESK

West Germany were preparing, in the autumn of 1950, for their first international match since the end of the war, and national coach Sepp Herberger was wrestling with the problem of whether to play perhaps his best player, Fritz Walter, who had been trying to overcome a knee injury for some weeks.

As he wasn't able to visit the player, Herberger had been phoning him regularly to check on him, but knew that Walter would be inclined to overestimate his level of fitness.

So, during a phone conversation with him days before the game, when he knew the player was sitting down near the desk on which his phone was placed, Herberger suddenly demanded: 'Please kick your desk rather hard, Fritz!'

Surprised, Walter did so, but Herberger said: 'I didn't hear anything. Kick harder!'

Walter did so, damaging his desk in the process, whereupon Herberger asked him: 'Are you having trouble with the knee now?'

Walter, still wincing, admitted, 'You bet' and was promptly dropped from the squad. West Germany won the game against Switzerland 1-0.

172. MAINTAINING STANDARDS

On the eve of the 1986 World Cup, FA chairman Bert Millichip issued instructions to the England squad that they should play at all times with their socks pulled up, and their shirts tucked into their shorts.

'I will also tell them that they should not be over-exuberant in celebrating their goals during the World Cup,' he announced.

173. NO CHANGE THERE, THEN

Manchester United star and Argentinian international Carlos Tevez has distinctive looks, including lank hair, broken teeth and a noticeably large scar on his neck.

He revealed that the teeth were broken 'in a street fight in a row over money' and the scar made when 'I had boiling water spilt on me. It was a defining experience – it marked me for life'.

Tevez also revealed in an interview with *Sport* magazine in March 2008 that 'when I started out playing for All Boys (as a youngster) I used the surname Martinez, which is my mother's name. That's the normal thing in Argentina for boys who are hoping to become football stars. They don't use their father's name because then it's easier for the big clubs to sign them without having to pay too much – you make it to the top by changing names.'

174. JEWEL PURPOSE

A 'radical jeweller' known only as 'Timothy', a fan of Derby County, held an exhibition of his work at London's Royal National Theatre in November 1998.

Among the items on sale were £36 badges, featuring phrases like 'You're sh*t, AHHH' and 'You fat bas*ard' while, available on special offer for just £12 from the Nottingham Forest-hating jeweller, was another, declaring 'Forest are sh*t'.

175. MACKIE'S MONKEY

Signed for Arsenal from a Belfast side in 1923, full-back Alex Mackie celebrated the move in flamboyant style, splashing out his first week's wages – about a fiver – on a pet monkey, 'to satisfy a life-long ambition'.

176. KISSED OFF

Ramon Moya, coach of Spanish 3rd Division side Hospitalet, could not conceal his joy when his side scored an injury-time winner in November 1998.

Moya promptly celebrated by kissing the nearby linesman on the cheek – for which he was promptly booked and, as he had already been yellow-carded, dismissed.

★ Alessandro Veronese was suspended for two matches for 'unusually intimate' actions after being sent off during a 1996 Italian non-league game for Battaglia – and then kissing the female referee who had red-carded him.

177. WHO'S NOT EATING ALL THE PIES?

After feeling humiliated when she became stuck in an Old Trafford turnstile while going in to see her favourite team, Manchester United, play during the 2005/06 season, 33-year-old Lisa Rea vowed to lose weight.

And she was so successful that within two years she had shed an amazing 16 of the 26-stone bulk that had seen her forced to wear an XXXL replica United shirt.

'Before, I couldn't even fit in my seat. I'd get bruises because I'd force myself through the turnstiles by wiggling about,' she said.

Eventually, Lisa took drastic action and underwent an operation to staple her stomach, which drastically reduced her appetite and capacity to eat: 'I see other fans eating pies and I feel physically sick.' With the money she has saved by not eating as much, taxation officer Lisa now pays for her season ticket.

178. HOSTAGE TO FORTUNE

When 46-year-old John Brooke was freed after being held hostage by gunmen in the Yemen in 1999, he told his liberators that he needed to make an urgent phone call – to find out how Norwich City had got on.

His wife, Katherine, was able to give him the news he feared most – Norwich had squandered a two-goal lead to lose 3-2.

179. NOT WORTH THE TIME OF DIA

The Times Online carried out a survey of supporters to discover the 50 worst players ever to appear in the English top flight. When the results were unveiled in July 2007, Southampton players occupied 50th and first positions.

At number 50 was Scandinavian Claus Lundekvam, of whom manager Gordon Strachan reportedly said: 'He was carried off at Leciester and someone asked me if he was unconscious. I didn't have a clue. That's what he's always like.' And in the coveted number-one spot was a man who arrived at Southampton with a reputation suggesting that he had 12 caps for his country, Senegal, and had played for Paris St Germain.

Ali Dia, also said to be the great George Weah's cousin and to have been recommended to the club by that all-time footballing legend, made his debut in 1996, showing almost no trace of footballing ability.

After 52 minutes, Graeme Souness hauled him off – and he never appeared for the club again.

180. LINCOLN FOR HEIFER

A 1991 advertisement in the *Grantham Journal* invited readers to ring about '11 Lincoln Red Heifers for sale' – and listed a phone number, which turned out to be that of the then underachieving Lincoln City FC.

181. SHAKY EXCUSE

Lazio defender Jose Antonio Chamot was sent off by referee Pierluigi Collina – for shaking hands with him.

It happened in April 1998 after Lazio's 1-0 defeat by Juventus, and Chamot was banned for one match after the handshake was construed as 'evident dissent'.

182. OARSOME DECISION

Fans had to get up early when the 1873 FA Cup final between Wanderers and Oxford University was scheduled for an 11am kick-off – so that players would be able to watch the University Boat Race afterwards.

Oxford lost both.

183. INJURY PRONE

★ Mo Johnston, then of Rangers, ricked his back after hurling mud in frustration when he missed a chance during a 1991 match at Aberdeen.

★ Duncan Jupp of Wimbledon was staying at a health centre in 1999 when he crashed his golf buggy into a tree and needed stitches in a head cut.

* Alan Mullery, formerly of Spurs and England, injured his neck while shaving and missed out on another cap.

* Robbie Keane suffered a knee injury that required an operation after he bent down to pick up his TV remote control.

* Bojan Tripic, Bosnia-Herzegovina league leaders Modrica's keeper, suffered severe burns in 2008 when attempting to throw a flare off the pitch.

* Charlie George, Arsenal legend, lost his leg end when he cut off his big toe with a lawnmower.

* Dave Beasant, Wimbledon keeper, severed tendons after dropping a jar of salad cream on his foot.

* Michael Stensgaard, Danish keeper at Liverpool in the mid-1990s, injured his shoulder trying to stop an ironing board falling over.

184. MISTAKEN IDENTITY

Alex Ferguson became Swindon's oldest player in November 1947 when he turned out, aged 43 years and 103 days. Then in 2000, Alex Ferguson received an 84-day suspension from the Middlesex County FA after 'head-to-head butting' during a Staines Lammas FC match.

* Michael Owen was introduced in January 2000 to the Archbishop of Canterbury, who was delighted to make the acquaintance of the bishop from Oklahoma.

* Kevin Keegan was fined £300 for 'frightening shoppers' on the day of the England-Scotland Euro 2000 qualifier. The 22-year-old claimed 'it was a case of mistaken identity'.

* Louis Enrique, the Barcelona superstar, was spotted at a Liverpool-Leeds match during the 1999-2000 season – except that it transpired he was actually Louis Emerick, an actor from TV's *Brookside* soap opera.

* Derided by the media during his tenure in the England managerial role as a 'turnip', it would appear that Graham Taylor, now frequently heard as a pundit for BBC Radio Five Live, is rather more highly regarded in America, where the Chicago Theological Seminary boasts a Graham Taylor Chapel and Hall.

* Julia Roberts, presumably moonlighting as tea-lady at Unibond League side Droylsden between acting gigs, was put in charge of the side when their form faltered during the 1999-2000 season – she and colleague Stella Quinn duly picked the side for their Manchester Premier Cup replay against Alder Hey, and their line-up produced a 2-1 win.

* Peter O'Sullivan, a 35-year-old bricklayer, in April 1966 named his new-born daughter Paula St John Lawrence Lawler Byrne Strong Yeats Stevenson Callaghan Hunt Milne Smith Thompson Shankly Paisley O'Sullivan. Guess which team he supported?

* Bob Hope was a Scottish player who turned out for WBA, Birmingham and Sheffield Wednesday in the 1970s.

185. APRIL FOOL

West Brom star Fabian Defreitas turned up in good time for his side's evening kick-off against Crewe in April 1999.

The game had started at 3pm and they lost 5-1 without him. He was fined.

186. HERBOOT CHAPMAN

Perhaps Arsenal's most famous manager – certainly before Arsene Wenger – was Herbert Chapman, whose playing career for Spurs and others early in the 1900s had been notable only for the fact that he wore bright yellow football boots. No-one seems to have recorded where or how he got them, but I imagine he did not use the method I adopted in the 1960s of painting his boots that colour.

My cunning plan to be the first local player to turn out in unusually coloured footwear foundered somewhat when I used a tin of gloss paint to effect the change from black to orange, only to discover that this rendered them singularly unable to bend.

Chapman signed a player for Arsenal at a fee of £3,900 – when they could have had him for 55p. Charlie Buchan had been at the club in 1909 but quit when they refused to reimburse him the 11 shillings expenses he had incurred while playing four reserve team matches.

187. NUN TOO LIKELY

Paul 'Gazza' Gascoigne (once heard to remark: 'I never predict anything and I neverl will do.') revealed one of the unexpected perils of becoming a Lazio player during his stay with the Italian club. He claimed that after a draw with local rivals Roma, he was attacked by nuns.

'Never had anything like it – nuns,' said Gazza. 'Roma supporters, giving us punches on the arms. I thought nuns were nice. Incredible. Getting punched by nuns.'

188. LOST A TENNER

Taxi driver Graham Jenkins staked £10 on a 15-match accumulator bet. Fourteen of his selections won, leaving him with £117,000 going on to a game happening the next day. If that result went his way he would win £292,882.98.

The 56-year-old Bournemouth man needed Raith to win at Airdrie on January 27, 1997, to clinch his winnings.

He refused to put any money on the two other possible outcomes of the game – known as 'hedging the bet', which would have guaranteed a profit regardless of the outcome.

'What's the point?' he asked. 'If it wins, it wins. If it loses, it loses.'

Airdrie had a player sent off before they crashed to a 4-1 defeat. Philosophical Mr Jenkins figured that he'd only lost a tenner.

189. PLAYING A BLINDER

Scottish international Jimmy Lang, born in 1851 and who played for Third Lanark and Sheffield Wednesday, had a unique claim to footballing fame.

Following an eye injury, which he suffered in the Clydebank shipyards, he became the only recorded professional footballer to be officially registered as blind.

190. CROSS DRESSER

Italian ladies' side Sora had a problem before a 1999-2000 match, so their male trainer, Piero Pucci, volunteered to step in as goalkeeper, trying – unsuccesfully as it transpired – to disguise himself courtesy of a wig and a bra containing two oranges.

191. MAC BOOKED

Isle of Wight Sunday League player Ian Dyer, 23, striker for Columbia, was yellow-carded as he walked on to the pitch in March 2000 for a game against Three Crowns and subsequently fined £6 – for eating a McDonald's Egg McMuffin.

192. THAT'S IT, I'M OUT OF HERE

Experienced Belgian UEFA referee Amand Ancion quit the game in tears after deliberately ruling out a legitimate goal during a domestic First Division game between Mouscron and Charleroi in March 2000.

The goal was scored when Charleroi's Biondo was down injured. Instead of kicking the ball out of play as sporting etiquette demanded, Mouscron's Lawaree carried on and scored – whereupon Ancion ruled the effort out on moral grounds, before then announcing he was quitting in disgust as a result.

193. DRIVEN TO IT

The small mystery of why Galatasaray player Ergun wore the number 67 on his shirt during their victory over Arsenal in the 2000 UEFA Cup final was eventually solved. No, it wasn't a superstition, nor a mystically significant number.

The answer was far more prosaic. Ergun revealed it represented the car registration code for the district of Turkey in which he lived.

194. WE'D BETTER CHANGE THE TIME

Fans rushed to buy tickets for Stoke's prestigious July 2000 friendly against Liverpool, scheduled for a 3pm kick-off – until a less than pleased local couple, Louise Collett and Kevin Whitehurst, pointed out that their wedding reception at the Britannia Stadium, booked a year earlier, clashed with that time.

Red-faced club officials had to reschedule kick-off for 12.30pm.

★ When Norwich fan Paul Murrell married Alison in 1986 their reception featured not a disco, but the commentary from Norwich's vital league match against West Ham.

195. SHORT OF BREAD

Cash-strapped Aberdeen needed to take drastic steps to reduce costs before the start of the 2000-01 season.

In a masterstroke they reduced their outgoings of dough – by removing the players' toaster, thus making an estimated saving per annum of £6.20.

★ In 1998-99 Portsmouth went into administration and among the money-saving measures introduced was to wash jockstraps. 'We were having new jockstraps for every game, so I said why not wash the damn things?' asked administrator Tom Burton, reasonably enough.

196. OH, YOU MEAN ME?

Even the most poorly educated of players is usually capable of spelling his or her name – but one high-profile England international discovered in February 2000 that he had been spelling his wrong for years: well, since he could spell, in fact.

Spurs defender Jonathon Woodgate had always spelled his name just like that – so it came as something of a shock when he found his birth certificate and noticed that on there he was Jonathan Woodgate!

★ Kevin Keegan's real first name is Joseph; Alan Curbishley's is Llewellyn; Jimmy Floyd Hasselbaink's is Jerell; Mark Hughes's is Leslie; Shaun Goater's Leonardo; former Leicester keeper Pegguy Arphexad's first name really is Pegguy – 'It's a girl's name in France, too, and I have no idea why I am called Pegguy,' he said in January 2000. 'You will have to ask my mother.'

197. EARLY BATH?

Newcastle striker Roy Bentley fell out with the club over the state of the bath in the flat belonging to the sister of a club director, where he was living in 1947.

'Get me a new bath,' demanded Bentley.

'No, we'll put a fresh coat of paint on the old one,' said the club.

Bentley left Newcastle for Chelsea in an £11,000 transfer.

198. BOOKED FOR FAILURE?

Football Impetigo was the title of Henry George Armstrong's 'enquiry into a contagious affection of the skin occurring amongst football players', published in 1896.

Christ on the Football Field propagated the Christian doctrine when it was published in 1913.

Soccer For Suckers (of what was not specified) was a 1960 book by Dennis Barry Jackson, published by Right Way Books.

El Tel was a Space Alien was a 1989 book by Martin Lacey about fanzines.

The Biological Evolution Of Football Club Names by Steve Spartak, published in 1993, claimed to have traced Bristol Rovers' name to an odd derivation – 'Brie's Tool Offers'.

199. YOU OLD ROMANTIC, YOU

Lanky 6ft 7in striker Kevin Francis, at Stockport County from 1991-95, proposed successfully to his girlfriend Sharon – through the club programme.

200. GOING THROUGH THE CARD

Having been shown the red card during a 1990 Italian amateur league game, Fernando D'Ercoli of Pianta snatched the card from the referee – and ate it.

201. CROSS PURPOSE

West Ham's inside right, Stan Earl, collapsed on the pitch during a Good Friday game in the mid-1920s, complaining of excrutiating stomach pains.

Fearing appendicitis, the club medics checked the England international anxiously, until he confessed that he was suffering from indigestion brought on almost certainly as a result of stuffing himself with FOUR hot cross buns as a pre-match treat.

202. DUGOUT DON

Every ground has some sort of construction described as a dugout, albeit they are usually nothing of the sort.

However, credit for the dugout should properly be given to the slightly eccentric

Aberdeen FC coach of the 1920s, Donald Colman, a boxing and dancing enthusiast keen to study at close quarters the footwork of his players.

In order to watch the game from pitch level, Colman had a sunken, covered area created alongside the pitch in (say some reports) 1923, which also had the benefit of allowing him to keep the notebook in which he scribbled down his observations on the proceedings dry and away from the elements.

Everton liked the look of the innovation when they visited Pittodrie – the first all-seater stadium in Britain – for a friendly, and they took the idea back with them and introduced it to the English game.

Dugouts inspired a book of that name by David Bauckham, published by New Holland in 2006.

203. STRETCHERED OFF

A pitch invader was carried off on a stretcher during a 1999 clash in South Africa between Premier League sides Mother City and Classic of Tembissa in Cape Town.

That was the only way they could eventually remove the mole, which had refused to leave the goalmouth until being enticed on to the stretcher.

204. LATE DEVELOPER

At the age of 52, Doncaster chairman John Ryan finally achieved his ambition in April 2003 when he made an appearance for the club – coming on as a very late sub in the 2-4 win at Hereford. He was on for one minute.

'I didn't actually get to kick the ball,' he said.

205. BLAME GAME

When West Ham were forced to replay their December 1999 Worthington (League) Cup quarter-final match against Aston Villa which they had already won once, boss Harry Redknapp was confident that it was not his fault.

Harry had brought on, as a 112th minute sub, the 21-year-old Manny Omoyinmi. He barely touched the ball and only watched as West Ham prevailed in a penalty shoot-out.

However, it seemed to have escaped Omoyinmi and everyone else at the club that he had already played in the competition earlier that season, when he was out on loan at Gillingham.

And Harry had given permission for him to play in the competition, but pointed out, reasonably enough (to 'Arry, anyway), 'There's a difference between giving permission and actually knowing he's played.'

Harry certainly wasn't about to blame 'the kid', though. 'I'm not going to blame the kid. I asked him why he didn't say anything and he said he didn't think,' said Harry in what clearly could in no way be described as a statement blaming the kid.

Not only that, Harry came up with another 'reason' why the club should not have the win taken away from them: 'Why should 26,000 people who love this football club have to suffer for a slight oversight by somebody? It's very harsh.'

Club officials in the secretaries' office tendered their resignation.

In the replayed game Villa were beaten 3-1.

But of course, no-one at the club blamed the kid – who was almost immediately sent out on loan to Scunthorpe. Then to Barnet.

Still not blaming him, they then transferred him at the end of the season to Oxford United, where Omoyinmi was later reported as saying: 'In the end, I just had to go. It was difficult on me and my family and it really hurt at the time. It's not nice reading nasty things written about you in the papers or said on TV. But I'm trying to move on now. I don't want to keep looking back.'

Still, at least he knew the Hammers didn't blame him for what had happened.

206. IF YOU EVER SAW HIM ...

Perhaps the most noteworthy of football club mascots is the Portland Timbers' talisman since 1977, Jim Serril – a man who became official mascot to the team after he and his brother brought chainsaws into the ground, with which they sawed great slabs of wood from local timbers to celebrate goals.

Leaving aside the reaction of health and safety officials if anyone even dreamed of such a thing in Britain, 'Timber Jim', as he became known, even abseiled from the stadium roof, wielding the chain saw.

Timbers fan Shawn Levy, with masterful understatement, said: 'The first time you see Timber Jim climb the 80ft Douglas Fir in the corner of the field without a ladder and then stand there, dance and beat the hell out of a drum for 20 minutes, it is just astounding.'

Not everyone was a Timber Jim fan and he was knocked cold by a bag of ice at a game in Vancouver where: 'I was in their face, I incited a riot. The next thing I know, I'm being escorted out of the country by the Canadian police.'

55-year-old Jim announced his retirement from the position in 2008 – perhaps he'd fancy a trip to Kenilworth Road to work alongside our 'Happy Harry'!

207. RUN IT OFF

Run it off was the advice of my teammate Dave Furlong, acting as physio on the day, to the apparently injured Jim Dickson, during a Hendon Sunday League game in the mid-1970s.

Dave's advice came with the benefit of the expertise acquired from a recent first aid course.

Jim did his best to comply with the instruction – not easy when you've broken your leg.

Billy Marsden, former Sheffield Wednesday player, would have empathised with Jim. Marsden was playing for England against Germany in May 1930 when, after 20 minutes, he collided with a teammate.

The trainer told Marsden to carry on, which he did until half-time – when the pain from what was a broken cervical verterbra proved too much.

The injury ended his career. Jim Dickson played again – no thanks to Dave Furlong!

208. WHY THE DINNER JACKET?

England skipper Terry Butcher reacted to criticism from manager Bobby Robson of his players' sartorial standards by attending a team meal wearing a dinner jacket and jockstrap. And nothing else.

The ultra-patriotic Butcher, capped 77 times, whose mobile phone reportedly rings to a heavy metal riff, and famous for coming off the pitch wearing a blood soaked headband and shirt after one match, surprised the footballing world when he joined the Scotland managerial team in 2008 after newly appointed boss George Burley invited him to do so.

209. DYING ART

Argentinian club Boca Juniors were overwhelmed by requests from the relatives of deceased supporters to allow their ashes to be scattered at the club.

So, in early 2008 they announced that they were opening their own supporters' graveyard and cemetery, with space for 27,000 fans.

Supporters often carry out their own impromptu ceremonies at the ground for dead fans – throwing plastic bags full of ashes on to the pitch during goal celebrations.

210. MONKEYING AROUND

Dorchester Town's newly appointed director broke new ground in February 1999, by being female.Oh, and by being a chimpanzee called Trudy.

Rescued from a local circus where she had allegedly been mistreated, the club made her an honorary board member.

★ The New York Cosmos mascot, a chimp called Harold, found himself in the monkey equivalent of the dog-house when he urinated over one of the club's players, Stanley Startzell, during a press conference.

211. BALLS OF BLASPHEMY

The US military came up with a plan to ingratiate themselves with the locals in Afghanistan when, during August 2007, they showered the area with footballs, dropped from a helicopter in Khost province.

So far, so good – except that some of the balls were adorned with designs, some featuring the Saudi flag, featuring the 'shahada', an Islamic declaration of faith that includes the name of Allah.

This did not go down well. 'To have a verse of the Koran on something you kick with your foot would be an insult in any Muslim country,' said Afghan politician Mirwais Yasini. Riots broke out and 100 people held a protest demonstration, reported BBC News.

212. DON'T BEE SILLY

Chic Brodie had been accident prone during his career, so perhaps becoming a cabbie when he retired in the early 1970s was asking for trouble.

Sure enough, former Brentford keeper Brodie's cab collided with a white Jaguar – driven by England's World Cup hat-trick hero, Geoff Hurst.

Chic had been forced out into the world of real work when, in November 1970, he collided during a game with a sheep-dog who had run on to the pitch, sustaining a serious leg injury.

During another match, Chic watched in astonishment as the goalposts collapsed around him while playing at Lincoln.

In November 1965, Chic was playing in goal for Brentford when one of the visiting Millwall fans threw a hand grenade in his direction.

Not quite sure what the object was, Chic picked it up and threw it in the back of his net – but then had second thoughts, looked more closely, and ran to the touchline to alert everyone.

The game was halted while the police were called and the grenade taken away.

It was eventually revealed to be a replica.

213. EXCUSE ME, YOU'RE ON THE LIST

'If you're driving to work then don't get in a car with Liam Miller. He gets involved in more car crashes than anyone I know,' declared Sunderland manager Roy Keane in February 2008.

But he wasn't really suggesting that the midfielder was a lousy driver – more that the Irish international was an excuse machine who was always exasperating his boss by being late for training.

'There's a different excuse each time, but we gave him the benefit of the doubt five, six, maybe seven times,' added Keane, confirming that he was transfer-listing the former Manchester United player.

214. GEORGEADONA?

During the Second World War, with much of football temporarily shelved, a substitute for the FA Cup, the two-legged Football League Cup (North) was played, with the 1944 finalists emerging as Blackpool and Aston Villa.

Blackpool took a 2-1 lead into the second leg at Villa Park in front of a 55,000 crowd.

The game was closely contested, with Villa eventually prevailing 4-2 to take the trophy. But their second goal definitely should not have been awarded – as an unrepentant George Edwards of Villa boasted after the game: 'Yes, I punched it in.

'There I was facing an open goal when I was pulled down from behind. As I fell, the ball bounced up so I gave it a mighty right-hander. It went in like a rocket and you could have heard a pin drop when the ref gave a goal. Everyone else knew I had handled it.'

So much for standards of honesty in the 'good old days'!

215. TOP SAINT

Southampton fan Richard Becheley, 25, of Locks Heath in Hampshire, revealed in February 2008 that he had collected 215 Southampton FC shirts.

216. ELSTRUP'S IN LAR-LAR LAND

Lars Elstrup was Luton Town's £650,000 record signing – perhaps that is what pushed the Danish international over the edge, and into areas perhaps beyond mere eccentricity.

In 1993, two seasons after being Luton's top scorer, and then returning to play in Denmark, he gave up football to join a religious sect, The Wild Goose commune, based on the island of Funen, where he was given a new name, Darando. 'I feel that here I am seen for who I really am. They understand me better than I do myself,' he said. But not many understood when he turned up in, and defecated upon, London's Trafalgar Square in July 2001.

He had returned to the public eye when, in the mid-1990s, he was seen in the middle of a busy pedestrianised shopping street in Copenhagen, circled by a rope and waving his private parts at passers-by.

'I do this to provoke people,' he commented, reasonably enough. 'I like experiencing people's reactions. Some might take my message to be 'sod off' and others an offer of sex. I love the fact that people recognise me as Lars Elstrup.'

He moved on to Odense, performing the same actions and being heckled by shoppers, after which he lost his temper and allegedly slapped a laughing schoolboy (with what is not reported), and wrestled with a police officer, before being arrested.

This behaviour was apparently too much even for his brethren in The Wild

Goose who expelled him – 'They are inhuman and even stole Devi, my dachshund,' complained Lars. 'I am now ready to go to the European Court of Human Rights.'

He did try to get back into football in 2000, playing in the Danish Amateur League.

Born in 1963, Elstrup played 34 matches, scoring 13 goals, for Denmark and was part of the side that won the 1992 European Championship.

Lars's own website shows photographs of him in some odd poses, in some of which he appears naked, and declares that 'he works with healing the Self, personal development, obtaining higher levels of consciousness, and sees man as being an energy'.

It is not known whether he is a friend of David Icke.

217. YAWN ALL

Crystal Palace and Reading played out what cannot have been an over-exciting 1-1 draw in October 1954, after which it was reported that a spectator had been taken to hospital after yawning so widely that he had suffered lockjaw.

218. FOR PETE'S SAKE

Police took exception when Swindon's PA announcer Pete Lewis decided at half-time to lay into the referee's performance in their April 1995 match against Bolton.

A senior officer cautioned Lewis, whose misery was completed when, after a 0-1 defeat, he was sacked from his position.

219. TAYLOR-MADE SPAT

Not unnaturally, Wolves boss Graham Taylor took offence when a fan spat at him following an April 1995 3-3 draw at Sheffield United.

Taylor attempted unsuccessfully to make a citizen's arrest.

Four days later, Blades fan Robert Hollister admitted to the offence and, following his release on bail after being questioned by the law, travelled to Molineux to apologise personally to Taylor.

220. FRYING TONIGHT

Albanian football fan Vilson Alushi was so convinced that his national team would beat Holland in their September 2007 match that he vowed to set light to the fishmonger's van in which he carried out his business if they failed to do so.

When the Dutch predictably enough proved too strong for the Albanians with a 0-1 win, Alushi was true to his word and duly set the fish van ablaze in the centre of the town of Delvine, fully expecting the fire service to quickly douse the flames.

The firefighters turned up and unleashed their hoses – only to discover that thirsty locals, suffering from the ongoing chronic water shortage in the area, had drained their water tanks.

221. ONCE A BOSS, ALWAYS ...

Neil Warnock, never far from controversy as a football manager, decided to watch his daughter, Amy, playing in an under-11 netball tournament in February 2008 – only to find himself giving the side a team talk after they drew their first game.

They won their next match, before coming up against the favourites. 'Another team talk must have inspired them as they won to reach the semi-final,' recalled Warnock in his *Independent* column.

They won again to reach the final, but by then 'I was absolutely freezing. I went to the car to thaw out, only to get a call saying "they're losing, get back here".'

Warnock rushed back 'and started shouting at the girls individually. We [note, that Neil has now become part of the team!] turned the deficit around to a 3-1 victory.'

222. THEY WENT TO THE MATCH – AND A REVOLUTION BROKE OUT

The story of the war that broke out between El Salvador and Honduras after qualifying games for the 1970 World Cup between the two has been told many times.

But few know of the more obscure case of a revolution that was inspired by a football match.

The match took place in Lucca, Tuscany, in April 1920 when that walled city's team played Sporting Club Viareggio in a local derby. The away side's supporters were welcomed with 'hostility and violence', it was reported.

The return fixture in May saw the Viareggio fans looking for revenge – to the extent that few Lucca fans travelled to the game, which was being refereed by a Lucca-based official who showed apparent bias to his home-town team.

One of the linesmen was Viareggio war hero Augusto Moranti.

When Lucca rallied from two down to draw level, home fans accused the ref of assisting them – and he promptly ended the game early.

Now the players began to fight each other whereupon a pitch invasion took place, sparking 'an enormous fight'.

Military police present helped save the Lucca players from the home fans, pushing Viareggio supporters outside the ground, where they regrouped and prepared to storm back in.

Attempting to restore order, a policeman fired a shot, killing linesman Moranti and enraging further the already irate crowd.

The caribinieri now made a strategic withdrawal of their own, while the Lucca players and fans fled town.

With no-one to fight, the Viareggio supporters decided to attack the barracks to get at the policeman who shot Moranti. They surrounded the police HQ, put up barricades and cut electricity lines, effectively leaving the town in the hands of a mob, which was rapidly boosted by the arrival of local anarchists who saw the opportunity to implement a revolution against the authorities.

It took several days and three military columns to quell the disturbance and re-establish the rule of law.

The two teams played a 'peace match' in 1921, to try to prevent ill-feeling escalating, but during the 1921-22 season violence again broke out during the derby matches between the two clubs.

223. CZECH THIS OUT

Jan Skorkovsky, a Czech, ran the entire distance of the 1990 Prague marathon playing 'keepy-uppy' with a football that never once touched the ground.

It took him 7hrs 18min 55sec.

Why, you may ask, is he not a professional footballer? Well, obviously, because he is actually a vet.

Don't believe it? Czech him out at www.skorkovsky.com!

224. WELL, ALBY DAMNED

I am indebted – and so should you be – to Michael Joyce, for the fascinating information that in all of the Football League matches played between 1888 and 1939, there were 1,115,364 'player appearances'.

And of that number, just one belonged to left-half Albert Smith of Loughborough Town, whose entire career may have been the most ignominious of any of the 16,151 players involved – consisting of a single match in March 1900, which resulted in a 12-0 defeat.

Mind you, at least his one game was for his own team. Derby County once played at Everton and arrived with only ten men, whereupon the hosts loaned them one of their players, Harboard, who played at right half, making his only career appearance – for another club! What's more, he ended up losing 6-2 to his own team.

How many goals do you reckon there were in those 50,700 matches? 161,577.

225. BY GUM

Referee Luigi Fedele began to choke when he swallowed his chewing gum during an October 1996 match in Italy between Colico and Novate.

A fast-thinking spectator grabbed a linesman's flag, which he used to prise open the ref's mouth before freeing his respiratory tract.

When he came round Fedele abandoned the match.

226. NET RESULT

Paraguay's star player Roberto Acuna had to be coaxed back into the national squad via a televised plea from coach Ever Almeida, after he walked out of the side during the 1999 Copa America – because the team doctor had put him on an all-fish diet.

227. FIRED?

Neil Warnock arrived as manager at Sheffield United from Bury in late 1999 after claiming that fans from his previous club had threatened to set fire to his wife. 'To hear some fans dislike you so much they want to burn your wife is just sick,' said Warnock.

228. SORRY, DEAR

The Albanian media reported in 1998 that after an Albanian man gambled £1,500 that Croatia would beat France in the World Cup he couldn't raise the stake money.

So he handed over his wife to the man who accepted the bet from him.

229. THEY WALKED IT

Hard-up Crystal Palace fan Vinnie Elphick, from Bridgend in south Wales, walked for eight days to get to his club's April 2000 Division One game at home to Blackburn, which they won 2-1.

230. GREATEST SAVE?

Gordon Banks's incredible dive against Brazil; Colombia keeper Rene Higuita's infamous 'scorpion' kick clearance during a Wembley international against England; Bruce Grobbelaar's amazing 'spaghetti legs' tactics when saving a penalty – all have been nominated for the most outrageous goalkeeping moment.

But a fan of 19th century goalkeeper Arthur Wharton of Rotherham wrote to his local paper, the *Telegraph*, to enthuse over one of his remarkable efforts: 'In a match between Rotherham and Wednesday, I saw Wharton jump, take hold of the crossbar, catch the ball between his legs and cause three onrushing forwards to fall into the net.' I'd love to have seen that.

231. BUM DEAL FOR GILL

Bristol City physio Gill O'Shea was the medium of a unique deal in March 2000 when she allowed her backside to be sponsored by local company Kwik Move – 'I'm always bent over players with my bum in the air and the cameras always focus on it,' she explained.

∗ When Deal Town reached the 2000 final of the FA Vase all the players, manager Tommy Simpson and chairman Roy Smith celebrated by having the club crest tattooed on their rear ends.

232. PUB CRAWL

The entire Fiji squad was sent home from a tour to Australia four games early in 1995 after the players sneaked out of their team hotel and went on a nine-hour pub crawl through Sydney's red-light district.

233. WEBB'S COB

Mike Webb, vice-chairman of Devon FA side Topsham Town, was banned for three years in December 1999 after running on to the pitch during a game against Elburton and punching one of his own players in the face, breaking his nose.

234. LET ME SHOE YOU THE WAY

Athletic Bilbao believed they had pulled off a major coup by persuading former Blackburn Rovers star, Englishman Fred Pentland, to become their new manager in 1923.

On arrival the cigar-smoking, bowler hat-wearing former First World War internee gathered the players together for their first training session.

As they waited to hear about the top training techniques of the day, which they hoped would see them become the top team in Spain, he introduced himself and then proceeded to show them, er, how to tie their bootlaces properly. 'Get the simple things right and the rest will follow,' he explained.

Maybe some of today's teams should take a look at their bootlace tying, as Pentland led Athletic to win the Cup that season.

He left two years later, but returned in 1929 and then twice won league titles with them, becoming infamous along the way for the tradition that his players would trash his bowler hat at the end of victorious games by jumping up and down on it. He got through 20 a season.

235. IT'S ALL KICKING OFF

'Can you kick it?' was the message sprayed alongside six footballs chained to lampposts and trees in Berlin during the 2006 World Cup.

When passers-by took up the offer, they soon wished they hadn't as the footballs were filled with concrete.

Two men who kicked them broke toes and another suffered severe bruising.

Two members of an Austrian art group called Mediengruppe were arrested, but claimed that their performance art piece, which they described as a 'symbolisation of the mass phenomenon poured in concrete' had not been intended to cause injuries.

236. SPECIAL BRU

Paco Bru was one of the first characters to create an impression in Spanish football. Born in 1885, he played for Barcelona and Espanyol before retiring in 1917 and becoming a referee.

He was determined to take no nonsense when he was in charge of a game, explained author Phil Ball in his history of the Spanish game, *Morbo*. 'Before his first game in charge he is alleged to have walked into the dressing room and pulled out a Colt pistol. Saying nothing, he threw the gun on to a table and put on his refereeing gear.

'Once changed, he picked up the gun and stuffed it down his shorts, explaining to a player who had the temerity to ask, that he wished to "guarantee a pacific match".'

There were no reports of trouble during that or other games he controlled.

237. BEFORE COLLINA – LO BELLO

Pierluigi Collina is regarded as the doyen of Italian, if not world, referees. But long before the bald-headed (caused by alopecia) official made his impact on the game, Italy's most widely recognised and controversial arbiter was a gentleman named Concetto Lo Bello – popularly known as 'The Prince'.

Invariably immaculately turned out, tall with a neatly trimmed moustache and black, brylcreemed hair, he officiated at 328 Serie A games from 1954-1974, during which time he:

* Was struck on the head by a stone hurled at him during a 1957 game but carried on reffing regardless.

* Forced a public apology from the Juventus president when the club tried to have him barred from handling their games.

* Had bottles thrown at him from the crowd, was taunted by the chant 'Du-ce, Du-ce', referring to dictator Benito Mussolini, and was then trapped in the changing room for hours by angry fans after controversial decisions during a tense game between top two Fiorentina and Cagliari in October 1969.

* Was debated in the Italian parliament.

* Clashed regularly with Milan midfielder Gianni Rivera who said of him, after being red-carded in 1973: 'He does not referee games, he uses them as a stage on which to show off his show-off behaviour.'

* Introduced flamboyant hand signals to back up his decisions – on three occasions knocking players over while so doing.

* Sued Vicenza fan Walter Giuliani for defamation in 1969, after he repeatedly insulted him from behind the goal.

* Entered the political world while still a ref when he became a Christian Democrat parliamentary deputy in 1972 then, later, Mayor of Syracuse, his Sicilian home town.

* Was chased out of town by two cars full of irate fans after sending off two Turin players in 1971 and then having to be given a police escort off the pitch.

238. COLLINA'S APOLOGY

Collina, undoubtedly the world's top ref during the latter stages of his career, caused a sensation in 1997 when he first awarded, but then disallowed, a 'goal' for Inter Milan. Advised by his linesman to rule the goal out, Collina not only did so but then ran over to the dugout to explain his decision to Inter boss Roy Hodgson.

The referee and manager then shook hands.

Collina had an offensive banner removed before continuing with one game and once even made two teams swap ends to protect a keeper from the hail of missiles being projected in his direction.

239. NO-ONE LIKES ME – ER, I DO CARE.

It was reported in February 1995 that Peterborough keeper John Keeley was packing the game in at the age of 33 'because of verbal abuse from supporters' – whether his own, or the opposition's, was not made clear.

240. REF MIKE TAKING THE MICK?

Players and spectators were astonished to see referee Mike Reed apparently celebrating as Patrick Berger scored for Liverpool in their February 2000 win over Leeds.

The ref was called in by officials to explain himself and was reprimanded and removed from a forthcoming, high-profile TV game after freely accepting that he had been congratulating himself for playing an advantage that had permitted Berger to go forward and score.

241. CEEFSAX

Bruce Rioch discovered in November 1997 that he had been sacked as assistant QPR manager – by reading the news on Ceefax.

242. HOW LOW CAN YOU GO?

UEFA forced Spartak Moscow to replay their UEFA Cup match against Swiss club Sion in September 1997 – because they had discovered that the Russian side's crossbars were too low off the ground – by 4.7 inches.

Days later, the German FA ordered a match to be replayed, after ruling that a goal 'scored' by Sean Dundee for Karlsruhe in a 2-2 draw against Munich 1860 had crossed the line after the ref had blown for time.

243. RIO DRIVEN OUT

Set to become the youngest England cap since Duncan Edwards in 1955, then 18-year-old West Ham defender Rio Ferdinand was dropped by England manager Glenn Hoddle from his squad in September 1997 because he had been banned from driving after failing a breath test.

244. SHEEPISH

Croatian third division player Ivica Supe was unaware that the club sponsor, a local shepherd, had promised to reward him for every goal he scored by supplying him with a sheep.

So, when in March 2007 he notched his 16th goal for Zagora FC, he was a little surprised to arrive for training only to be greeted by a flock of sheep – his!

The 29-year-old said he had no idea where he would keep the animals and had the good grace to look sheepish.

245. ON YOUR BIKE, BOYS

Penarol fans were not best pleased that their side were trailing Danubio in a Uruguayan League match in June 1996 by 1-0. The fans began to pelt the pitch with rocks, bottles, coins and any number of other objects in an effort to get the game abandoned.

The ref refused to submit to this blackmail by barrage but when he looked round to see his linesman lying on the side of the pitch, having been felled by a motorcycle helmet, he admitted defeat and called the game to a halt.

246. 6-1 WIN? NOT GOOD ENOUGH!

Dundee United ran out easy 6-1 winners over Motherwell in their Scottish Cup quarter-final game in March 1981 – much to the disgust of manager Jim McLean.

He raged at his players for 'failing to entertain the paying customers' and then hit them where it really hurt – in the wallet. He fined them half of their win bonus, telling them that, having been 4-1 up at half-time, they had 'eased off'.

★ In 1962 a 6-2 scoreline was not good enough for Manchester City in their fourth round FA Cup tie at Luton Town – the game was abandoned after 69 minutes because the pitch was waterlogged. Denis Law had scored all six goals for City and was on target again when the match was replayed four days later – but this time Luton won 3-1.

247. WRONG REFS ARE ALWAYS RIGHT

Even though Alan Hudson's shot for Chelsea had hit the Ipswich side-netting during their First Division clash at Stamford Bridge, a goal was awarded.

On the same day, September 26, 1970, over at Leicester a Jim Storrie header hit the back of the net but somehow bounced back out during the game against Portsmouth. No goal was awarded.

Film and photographic evidence was produced to illustrate both cases but the decisions stood.

248. LOOKING TO THE FUTURE – AGED 91

August 12, 2007: 'I've done a hell of a lot in my life and in football, but there's still a lot more I want to do. I'll never give up my work. Never.'. Former Welsh international and Aston Villa skipper Ivor Powell, now assistant coach at British Gas Football League Premier Division side Team Bath, contemplating the future at the tender age of 91!

He was awarded the MBE later that year.

249. SICK AS THE PROVERBIAL

Tottenham Hotspur went on a tour of Argentina and Uruguay in 1909. On the cruise ship journey home a fancy dress contest was organised, and jointly won by two Spurs players, who dressed up as Robinson Crusoe and Man Friday, complete with a live parrot, which was supplied by ship officials who gifted the talking bird to the players concerned.

Almost exactly a decade later, deadly rivals Arsenal controversially replaced Spurs in the First Division – and on the very same day the parrot perished; expired;

became deceased; went to meet its maker ; pegged it; shuffled off this mortal coil; popped off; perished; died.

Consequently, Spurs were as sick as a ...

250. STRANGE THINGS ABOUT FOOTBALL WHICH IT WOULD BE STRANGE IF YOU DIDN'T KNOW ALREADY BUT WHICH ARE INCLUDED IN CASE SOME STRANGE PEOPLE THOUGHT IT STRANGE THAT THEY WEREN'T INCLUDED IN A BOOK ABOUT STRANGE FOOTBALL THINGS

* Nottingham Forest's Roy Dwight, who played, scored and broke his leg in the 1959 FA Cup final, was the uncle of Reg Dwight – alias Elton John.

* Manchester City's German keeper Bert Trautmann, a former prisoner of war, broke his neck in the 1955-56 FA Cup final, yet played on for the remaining 20 minutes.

* Manchester United's Carlos Tevez began celebrating his goals in January 2008 by removing from his shorts a baby's dummy, which the new father then sucked – it at least made a change from players spitting them out.

* Former England boss Steve McClaren, dubbed the 'Wally with a Brolly' after standing on the sidelines in the rain while England lost to Croatia and failed to qualify for Euro 08, confessed that he had been showered with umbrellas for Christmas 2007.

* Scotland international keeper James 'Joe' Kennaway of mid-1930s Celtic

already boasted international caps for his native Canada against USA, in 1928, and for USA against Canada, in 1930.

* Peter Knowles, England under-23 striker and brother of Spurs full-back Cyril, informed his club Wolves in August 1969 that he was giving up football to work full time as a Jehovah's Witness.

* England skipper Bobby Moore was arrested on a jewel theft charge on May 25, 1970 in Bogota where the squad were en route for the World Cup finals in Mexico. He was freed after being held for four days.

* Len 'Clown Prince of Football' Shackleton, a star player of the 1940s and '50s, entitled a chapter of his autobiography, 'The Average Knowledge of Football' – and left it blank. In 2002 Chumbawumba entitled an album track 'Song for Len Shackleton'.

* The most prolific season for footballers called Wilfred was 1935-36 when 20 of them played in Football League matches.

251. STRANGE QUIZ QUESTIONS

* Who was Scotland's first ever World Cup scorer? Kilmarnock-born Jimmy Brown – for USA versus Argentina in the 1930 semi-final.

* Name the PC who rode the legendary 'white horse' at the first Wembley FA Cup final in 1923? PC Scorey rode Billy.

* Which Scottish club has played Barcelona four times in competitive games – and won all four? In 1966 they played twice in the Fairs Cup, and in 1986 twice in the UEFA Cup – and Dundee United won all four matches.

* What is the unique contribution to football made by three Argentinians named Tossolini, Valbonesi and Polo? In the 1930s they invented the lace-free, 'valve-ball' football.

* Who was the first top division player to be heard declaring himself 'sick as a parrot' in a post-match interview? Liverpool's Phil Thompson after they lost 1-0 to Nottingham Forest in the replayed League Cup final on March 22, 1978.

* What was the significance of Gareth Roberts' 38th minute goal for Fulham at home to Tranmere in their Division One game in January 2000? It was the first own goal of the new century.

* What was unique about Paul Scholes's yellow card, received after scoring for England against Scotland in a Euro 2000 play-off game at Hampden Park? He was the first England international booked for over-celebrating a goal.

* What did Eric Cantona, Ryan Giggs and David Beckham achieve which no other Manchester United player ever managed? They all scored for United while wearing their controversial, short-lived grey kit, blamed by Fergie for one poor performance in which he claimed the players were unable to distinguish each other in the shirts.

* What was Fred Davies's unique contribution to British football over 45 years? He used his coracle to rescue balls kicked out of Shrewsbury's ground into the

River Severn, earning between 25p and 50p per ball – once retrieving 130 in a single season before retiring in 1986.

★ Who does Postman Pat support? Pencaster United.

252. STRANGE FOOTBALL CONNECTIONS

★ Between deceased Pope John Paul II, himself a goalkeeper, and well-travelled keeper Dean Kiely – one of whom wishes to return in a future life as the other.

★ Between movie murderer Hannibal Lecter and Julian Joachim, glimpsed playing for Leicester during the film, *Hannibal*.

★ Between Admiral Nelson and Blackpool FC – the naval legend is said to haunt the club's boardroom, where wood from Nelson's ship Foudroyant was used in panelling.

★ Between Gandhi and Gary Lineker? In early 2008 the people of Leicester were asked to choose between the two to be honoured by having their image displayed on a plinth in the city.

★ Between Gary Lineker and John Lennon? Both were given the middle name Winston, after Churchill.

★ Between Gary Lineker and Winston Churchill? Both were born on November 30.

★ Between Bert Turner of Charlton in 1946; Tommy Hutchison of Manchester City in 1981 and Gary Mabbutt of Spurs in 1987 – they all scored for both sides in the FA Cup final.

253. PARANOID, ME?

Glencraig United were preparing for their February 1975 local league game at their ground near Clydebank, Scotland.

Spirits were high and an informal sing-song had broken out, featuring a number of ditties making intimate reference to referees.

The sing-song coincided with the arrival of referee Mr Tarbet, who took immediate offence at the lyrics being sung, assuming them to be aimed at him – and he promptly booked all 13 Glencraig players and subs even before they had gone out on to the pitch.

254. WARREN'S PIECE OF THE ACTION

Barmouth & Dyffryn were ready to take on Real Llandudno in a Welsh league game in April 2007 when the referee pulled out with a sudden injury.

An appeal for a substitute official saw Anthony Warren, a qualified ref, step in to the breach.

Anthony had to borrow a kit but had brought his own whistle along. The game went off without incident as Barmouth won 9-2.

'They never gave me any trouble, they were all quite respectful,' said Anthony of the players.

Retired electrician Anthony was EIGHTY-TWO years old at the time.

255. WILMSLOW GIRL IS QUARTER-MILLION WINNER

Wilmslow woman Angela Kennedy was not best pleased when her husband and son went off to football matches, leaving her alone at home.

So she decided to take them on at their own game by proving to them that she knew something about football herself.

On March 31, 2006, she phoned bookies William Hill to place an accumulator bet with a £2,000 stake on NINE footballing eventualities – Manchester United finishing second in the Premiership; Sheffield United to finish second in the Championship; Southend to win League One; Carlisle to win League Two; St Mirren to win the Scottish First Division; Cowdenbeath to win Scottish Division Three; Liverpool to win the FA Cup; Hearts to win the Scottish Cup – and Grays Athletic to win the FA Trophy.

Every selection was successful – and Angela collected £242,391.66, the biggest winning football accumulator ever paid out to a female client.

256. BRAMALL BATTLE

The 'game' between Neil Warnock-managed Sheffield United and WBA 'played' at Bramall Lane on March 16, 2002 was abandoned after 82 minutes with the promotion-chasing Baggies 3-0 ahead – as United only had six players left on the pitch after three had been red-carded and two more taken off with injuries which, some believed, were less than career- threatening knocks!

With no more subs to bring on ref Eddie Wolstenholme had to call a halt, having also had to deal with a mass brawl on the pitch and a bust-up between the different sides in the dugout areas.

There was talk of a replayed game but Baggies boss Gary Megson insisted: 'If we are called back to Bramall Lane we shall kick-off – then walk off.'

Eventually the result was allowed to stand and United were fined £10,000. Two of United's red-carded trio, Santos and Suffo, never played for them again.

257. JUST YOU GET BACK HERE, NOW

Unlike ref Wolstenholme (see previous story), when Andy Hall was officiating in the September 2000 clash between Ipswich and Millwall and the visitors were reduced to seven players, he insisted on the bringing back of one of their apparently injured men.

The game had reached the final two minutes of extra time and Millwall, 5-0 down, had already had two players red-carded and used all their subs when Chris Kinet and Tim Cahill both limped off injured, after assistant manager Ray Harford called them off.

Birmingham official Hall stopped the game and demanded that Cahill come back on.

258. UNDENIABLY A DIRTY SIDE

Sam Allardyce was so upset at what he regarded as the below-par condition of the changing room to be provided for his Bolton side at Tranmere's Prenton Park for their August 2000 clash that he refused to let his players use the facilities.

Instead, they arrived at the ground 35 minutes before kick-off, already changed, and after the game they climbed straight back on the team coach and headed home without even showering.

The ill-feeling between Allardyce and John Aldridge-managed Tranmere stemmed from his disapproval of some of the tactics he believed Rovers employed to enable their long-throw specialist Dave Challinor to make the best of use of his speciality via assistance from ball boys, towels and relocated hoardings.

259. CHERRY-PICKING THE
PERFORMANCE-BOOSTING SUBSTANCES

'To Football Players' screamed the headline in an advertisement contained in an 1887 edition of the highly influential *Athletic News*. 'Athletes know that it is most important for them to take those foods which strengthen and invigorate the system. GRANT'S MORELLA CHERRY BRANDY has been proved to possess these necessary qualities.

'Captain Boynton used it whilst swimming the Straits of Dover. He wrote, "I found it not only palatable and refreshing, but most effective in keeping up both nerve and strength; under such circumstances again I would not be without it."

'Nothing is so comforting to spectators at football matches on a cold day as a nip of this delicious liqueur. It can be obtained at 3s 6d (17.5p) a bottle at all wine merchants, and retailed at all bars and restaurants.

'Beware of spurious imitations.'

260. PERFORMANCE-ENHANCING MONKEYS?

Manager at Wolves and Leeds, Major Frank Buckley fed his players a mysterious 'monkey gland treatment', the veracity of which was never fully established, despite questions being asked in the House of Commons and of the British Medical Association.

It seems likely that the small, brown capsules taken by Wolves players from the 1937-38 season, and later when he was at Leeds before their 1951 fourth round FA Cup defeat by Manchester United, were little more than placebos or, as some suggested at the time, anti-flu treatments.

Some years earlier, during the 1924-25 season, Arsenal players were given 'pep-pills' designed to supply them with 'extra punch and stamina' before a first round FA Cup game against West Ham.

It took three attempts to get the game played due to fog and when it was, ending in a 0-0 draw, the players had had enough of the pills which, said one, 'left a bitter taste, a raging thirst and pent-up energy for which there was no outlet'.

They refused to take them again.

261. EUROPE'S MOST RIGHT-ON CLUB

FC St Pauli, a Hamburg-based club playing just a division below the Bundesliga during the 2007-08 season, boasts a number of unique achievements and attributes – not least its unofficial skull-and-crossbones logo.

Formed in 1899, the club was first promoted to the Bundesliga in 1977, albeit for just one season.

But during the mid-1980s the club acquired its image of being a 'Kult' club. Based in the dock area of Hamburg close to the infamous Reeperbahn, the club became associated with politically left-leaning fans and became the first team in Germany officially to ban right-wing, nationalist activities and displays in the stadium, during an era in which fascist-inspired hooliganism was a problem.

St Pauli took an outspoken stance against racism, fascism, sexism and homophobia, embodying these matters in its constitution.

In 2002, conscious of having the largest number of female fans in German football, the club removed advertisements for men's magazine Maxim from the stadium after fan protests over sexist depictions of women. The club also has a women's rugby team.

In 2005 the club launched a charity appeal to raise money for water dispensers for Cuban schools.

Rock band front man Andrew Eldritch, of the Sisters of Mercy, is reportedly a supporter/sponsor of the club, whose players run out to AC/DC's 'Hell's Bells' before matches. The Blur track 'Song 2' is played every time the team scores, 'turning the stadium into a giant mosh-pit'.

The club is also very proud of having the last manual scoreboard in the higher divisions with a club official changing the score with number placards by hand.

St Pauli has frequently made pre-season appearances at a heavy metal festival, the Wacken Open Air.

In 2006 the club hosted the FIFI Wild Cup, a tournament for unrecognised national football representative sides such as Greenland, Tibet and Zanzibar, taking part themselves as 'Republic of St Pauli'. Northern Cyprus beat Zanzibar 4-1 in a penalty shoot-out in the final.

262. DELIA COOKED UP A STORM

Norwich had squandered a two-goal lead, allowing Manchester City to draw level by half-time in their February 2005 Premiership clash.

Even so, fans were astonished when their celebrity director, chef Delia Smith, strode on to the pitch during the interval, brandishing a microphone, and exhorting the fans to lift the side to victory.

'Where are you?' she shouted. 'Where are you? Let's be having you. Come on!'

Her strident tones and apparently eccentric attitude encouraged some misguided members of the crowd to surmise that perhaps Delia had been enjoying a libation – something she strenuously denied at the time and ever since.

The rallying cry did not have the desired effect as Norwich ended up losing the match 2-3.

After being criticised for an implied suggestion that the fans were being less than supportive, Delia admitted: 'Maybe in the heat of the moment I didn't choose the best words.'

As a gesture of reconciliation Delia sat with fans during the next match against Chelsea, even cuddling one who was clad in a fetching T-shirt bearing the phrase 'Let's be having you'.

263. EARLY ULTRAS

Italy's first organised football championship was held in Turin in May 1898 – in one day.

It was played out on a single pitch with Internazionale di Torino losing 2-1 to Genoa in the final in front of a crowd of just over 100. Among them were the type of elements who would later become known as 'ultras', the hooligan element that besmirches Italian football to this day.

Football historian Antonio Ghirelli says that the supporters 'fought briefly amongst themselves' and booed the ref, 'a habit which would continue'.

264. WHAT A SHOWER, THOSE ITALIANS

Apart from Juventus shirts being modelled on those of Notts County way back in the early days of Italian football, there are few things that the current World Champions are likely to acknowledge they owe to the English – but we know better.

Little known in his own country, but a legend of soccer in Italy, former Reading and Woolwich Arsenal player William Garbutt, then 29, became manager of Genoa in 1912 – the first professional boss appointed in Italy.

As well as introducing previously unheard of training techniques he gave the Italians that essential equipment – hot showers in the dressing room.

Garbutt is also believed to be the source of the still-used expression 'il mister' to denote the manager.

265. DIVORCED FROM HIS CLUB

Derby games between German sides Nuremberg and Furth were often marred by crowd violence in the early days of the game. Following a pitch invasion in 1910, things deteriorated to the extent that when in 1920 Furth's star player Hans Sutor married a girl from Nuremberg, he was forced out of his club.

266. THE FIRST DODGY KEEPER?

Aston Villa keeper Jimmy Warner was accused of betting against his club in the 1892 FA Cup final, and of then going out of his way to ensure his team lost.

Warner, who also ran a pub, defended himself at the time in an ambiguous statement, declaring: 'I wouldn't do such a thing for £1,000. I bet £18 to £12 against Albion winning and I even bet an even £1 that they would not score against me.'

Well, he certainly lost the bet about West Brom scoring, which they did after just four minutes from what was described as a 'soft' shot from winger Geddes, before they doubled the lead when Nicholls got to the ball ahead of Warner. And Villa were three down before the break when a long-range shot 'that Warner should have saved' somehow eluded him.

Warner blamed the over-confidence of his side for their defeat. 'So sure were the men of winning that they began to talk about who should engrave their names on the medals.'

Villa fans visited Warner's pub, not for a drink, but to accuse him of chucking the game – and Warner was seen receiving money from a known disreputable character, which he explained away as a small loan.

The Villa committee called a meeting to discuss Warner within four days of the final being played and he was immediately dropped, never to regain his place.

267. WHAT DID HE SAY?

Driving off to witness my team lose yet again in February 2008, I heard Fulham assistant boss Ray Lewington previewing his side's game at Craven Cottage against Manchester United that afternoon. And I am convinced that I did not mishear him.

'We have to start winning our home games,' he informed the interviewer, 'wherever we're playing.'

I immediately recalled Jamie Redknapp's comment a few days earlier about the England and Portsmouth keeper – 'What David James was guilty of, and it's not his fault, was coming for crosses.'

Titus Bramble, a talented but erratic defender, has been the bane of many bosses' lives – Sir Bobby Robson put his finger on why that is: 'Titus makes one mistake in every game. If he could just correct that bad habit, he would be one of the best defenders in England.' As statements of the bl**ding obvious, that takes some beating.

Another Newcastle icon, Kevin Keegan, evidently feeling the pressure as his side became involved in a relegation struggle in March 2008, declared: 'I'm 100 per cent committed to this club. You can't get more committed than that.'

268. JUST LIKE WATCHING ... URUGUAY

Alydr Garcia Schlee, a 19-year-old illustrator, won a competition in 1950 to devise a new strip for the Brazilian national side, which had lost the World Cup that year while wearing white shirts and blue collars.

He devised the now legendary, predominantly yellow strip, which they first wore in 1954 – but kept quiet the fact that he supported Uruguay, who beat Brazil in the 1950 World Cup final.

Brazil went on to win the 1958 World Cup, but didn't wear their yellow shirts in the final – as they clashed with hosts Sweden's colours.

269. BETHLEHEM BUST-UP

Few people are aware that football did not start in America when Pele went to play there.

Back in 1916 the game was already making inroads to the extent that there was a National Challenge Cup, which had launched in 1913, and attracted teams from as far west as Chicago and as far north as Niagra Falls – and it stirred up passions, too.

The 1916 Final saw a lively crowd of 10,000 flock to Pawtucket to see two of the big noises of the sport, Bethlehem FC, from 60 miles north of Philadelphia, and Fall River Rovers, from New England, who had made that stage from a starting line up of over 80 clubs.

The Pawtucket Evening times takes up the story with the game entering its final minute, with Bethlehem a goal up thanks to a controversial penalty; 'The Rover rooters, distinguished by the yellow cards in their hats, kept up a fearful din of disapproval. Suddenly, just as Referee Whyte was about to blow his whistle and end the game, a short, thick-set man was seen running out toward the centre of the field.

'That was all there was needed to precipitate a riot. In an instant the field was black with people, and Referee Whyte disappeared in a vortex of struggling humanity. The players formed a cordon about the official and, aided by the police, who used their clubs freely Whyte was dragged to the J & P Coats clubhouse, his shirt torn from his back and his body black and blue from the pummelling he received.'

270. J.LOW'S PILGRIMAGE

Scotland fan John Low travelled 7350 miles from his home in Castle Douglas to Mendoza, Argentina in June 2008 – so that he could recreate one of Scotland's most famous football moments thirty years on to the day.

John, in his fifties, recruited Argentinian office workers to act as Dutch defenders so that he could play out the role of Archie Gemmill, who scored a remarkable goal against Holland during the 1978 World Cup at the Estadio Malvinas.

'I just turned up on the day. I managed to track down the woman who was director of the sports complex – and she was suitably impressed by me wearing a kilt. All the people who worked in the stadium viewed me as a bit of an oddity. I needed people to be the Dutch defenders and goalie. I managed to persuade a few office workers.'

John donned a replica Scotland kit to reproduce the goal – and whilst he was doing so bumped into fellow Castle Dougals resident Jim Kentley – who went out for the World Cup in 1978 and liked the place so much he never went home.

271. A REICH CO*K UP

Swiss TV channel SRG flashed up the words to the German national anthem prior to the Euro 2008 finals match between Germany and Austria. However, they put up the words which were banned after the Second World War – 'Deutschland, Deutschland uber alles, uber alles in der Welt'.

After supporters watching on giant screens booed and threw beer and food, and complaints poured into the station the broadcaster claimed the words had been inadvertently copied from the internet.

Staff responsible were ordered to attend lessons on the Holocaust and German history.

272. MAKING A SPLASH

After 25 years without a title to their name, Standard Liege beat defending champions Anderlecht to win the Belgian League in 2008, resulting in Ecuadorean keeper, Rorys Aragon Espinoza jumping off a bridge wearing lycra and goggles, to celebrate.

Watched by hundreds of fans leaping into the Meuse river in Liege, he pledged to repeat the feat 'if we are champions next year'.

273. WHAT'S UP, DOC?

When Brazil travelled to their Gothenburg hotel to contest the 1958 World Cup, the team doctor was so determined that he would keep the team's minds on football and off other pursuits that he insisted on replacing their hotel's 28 female members of staff with male equivalents.

And he also persuaded a nearby nudist colony, visible from the hotel windows, to insist that members – sorry – remain clothed throughout the tournament.

Brazil beat Sweden 5-2 in the final.

274. ONE HELL OF A COMMENTARY

When Norway beat England in 1981, commentator Bjorge Lillelien was rather pleased – so much so that his rapturous outburst was, in June 2008, declared the 'Greatest bit of commentary. Ever' by the *Observer Sports Monthly*, which reproduced his words in full: 'Lord Nelson! Lord Beaverbrook! Sir Winston Churchill! Sir Anthony Eden! Clement Attlee! Henry Cooper! Lady Diana! Maggie Thatcher – can you hear me, Maggie Thatcher? Your boys took one hell of a beating!'

275. CZECH THIS OUT

The CzechFootball Federation apologised to the Lithuanian football authorities – after confusing them with Latvia.

Prior to their May 2008 clash the Czechs played the Latvian national anthem and featured pen pictures of the expected Latvia side in the match programme, alongside the Latvian flag

276. NOT SO ARMLESS

Striker Lee Thorpe missed Rochdale's League Two 1st Leg Play Off match against Darlington after breaking his arm – in an arm wrestling contest against a team-mate on the coach to the game.

277. TO ELLAND BACK

55 year old football hater Jane Lindley from Retford, Nottinghamshire, underwent a liver transplant after developing hepatitis C in 1999.

She received the organ from a young man from West Yorkshire,and after the operation suddenly found that she had become a passionate Leeds United fan.

'It's all very strange. I'm finding I'm thinking about Leeds United more and more. I know all the players' names and understand the game' she told the *Retford Times.*

278. WHAT ARE YOU TALCING ABOUT?

Top Brazilian club Fluminese's fans have an odd pre-match ritual, which involves the throwing in the air of talcum powder.

It originated as a tribute to the first mulatto to play for the club, one Carlos Alberto, the son of a photographer who, in 1914 (some say 1916), in an effort to appear paler skinned would whiten his face with rice powder – resulting in fans chanting 'Rice Powder' (po de arroz) at him – and leading to that becoming the club's nickname.

279. WE'RE FOXED

When holes a few inches across and of a similar depth appeared, groundstaff at Sheffield United's Bramall Lane ground were initially baffled in December 1999.

A clue emerged when it was discovered that leftover food seemed to have been buried in the holes.

'Who ate all the pies?' was the question asked by groundsman Glenn Northcliffe, who soon identified foxes as the culprits – and had to re-turf eight parts of the pitch.

280. DO YOU RECKON PELE'S SEEN THE FULL MONTY?

Actor Robert Carlyle, 46, star of movie *The Full Monty*, a married man with three children, declared in *The Guardian Weekend* of February 2008 that his most treasured possession is 'a Brazil top signed by Pele'.

281. HANDY KEEPER

TV presenter Jake Humphrey volunteered to face penalties from keepers Craig Gordon and Raimond van der Gouw when he visited Sunderland's training ground in February 2008 to record a spot for the *Sportsround* programme on BBC2.

The 29-year-old stepped between the posts as Gordon ran up and belted the ball towards him. Humphrey managed to get his hands to the ball, saving the shot – but breaking two fingers and spraining his wrist in the process.

282. WHAT'S IN A NAME?

'It could be worse – my dad's name was Roger, and his brother's name was Richard.' So said former Arsenal and England keeper David Seaman when quizzed by *The Times* about his surname – 'Seaman, as in sailor, that's what I always tell people,' he went on. 'I've always been a David. I've never liked Dave.'

283. BORN AND BRED

The 1913 meeting to establish a new football club in Dusseldorf, Germany had proceeded very well – until arriving at the point where the club had to be officially named.

Agreement could not be reached – until a vehicle passed by carrying the name of the local Fortuna Bakery. Fortuna Dusseldorf was named within minutes.

∗ Hertha Berlin were named after the pleasure steamer on which the club founders enjoyed a pleasant afternoon's sailing.

* The initial part of Borussia Dortmund's name came about after a meeting held in a beer-hall featuring an advertisement for the Borussia brewery.

* Bremen were called Werder because they played on a meadow next to a river, or a Werder. Good job they didn't play on a rubbish dump – although Frankenthal actually did!

284. WATCH IT, REF

It was revealed in early 2000 that Serie A side Roma's president, Franco Sensi, had given 41 Rolex watches to referees officiating at matches in the top Italian division.

'Roma wants nothing from referees. They are free to receive presents if they want. All the costs were declared and are included in Roma's budget. Everything has taken place in the open,' protested Sensi when a storm broke over the £1,800 – £8,000 timepieces.

Two of the recipients of the higher-priced watches announced they would keep them as 'if we had given the gifts back it would have led to more embarrassment and debate'.

What you might call a timely response.

285. DAZZLING PERFORMANCE

Cristiano Ronaldo was 'targeted' by a fan shining a green laser-pen light into his face during the warm-up and first half of Manchester United's 1-1 Champions League draw at Lyon in February 2008.

Medical opinions seem to be divided as to whether any ill-effects can accrue as the result of such treatment – although all seem to be agreed that green laser light is worse than red.

Sir Alex Ferguson reported the incident to UEFA, who seemed not to have any real ideas of how to deal with such an offence or even whether it needed dealing with.

286. HAD THEIR CHIPS

Chipstead trailed Epsom & Ewell by the only goal of their game in a Southern Youth League clash in February 2008 when the referee was forced to abandon the match midway through the second half – by seven police officers who roared up in three cars and then handcuffed and arrested four of the teenage Chipstead players.

They were taken away to a nearby police station for questioning about an alleged incident that had occurred while they were en route to the match, involving a near-miss in a car that had reversed very close to the players, who had reportedly not been best pleased to be almost run over.

The players were later released without being charged and Chipstead secretary Geoff Corner told the *Non-League Paper*: 'We really thought the police went over the top.'

287. SETTING AN EXAMPLE?

Newly appointed Secretary of State for Culture, Media and Sport, Andy Burnham, decided in February 2008 that he had better make a clean breast of his pitch invasion at Goodison Park when he was a much younger Everton fan: 'I invaded the pitch when Adrian Heath got his last-minute winner at Highbury.'

Asked by an *Independent* reader, Kevin O'Neill of Liverpool, whether he thought that fans 'who run on the pitch should be given a lifetime ban?', Burnham responded: 'I think there should be second chances for young lads, particularly Evertonians, who take part in good-natured pitch celebrations when they have suffered a childhood of disappointment up to that point!'

288. LONG SHOT OWN GOAL

Croatian fan Hrvoje Stanisic was beside himself with delight as his country beat Sweden 1-0 in their October 2005 World Cup qualifier.

Stanisic fired off his gun to celebrate – fatally shooting himself in the process.

289. HALF-HEARTED WINNER

Adrian Hayward, a Liverpool fan from Newbury, Berkshire, was so convinced that midfielder Xabi Alonso would achieve his ambition of scoring a goal from within his own half that he staked £200 on him doing so in July 2005 at odds of 125-1.

On January 7, 2006, Liverpool visited Kenilworth Road to play Luton Town in the third round of the FA Cup. With Liverpool 4-3 ahead Luton were making desperate efforts to equalise. Keeper Marlon Beresford had come up for a corner, which was cleared out to Alonso, who saw Beresford was struggling to get back to his area and hit a speculative long shot from within his own half. It found its way into the back of the net, putting Liverpool through, annoying me greatly, and winning Mr Hayward, 42, £25,000 – 'I've never placed such a large bet before but I had a feeling about it,' he said.

290. STRANGEST EXISTENTIAL DAMAGE

A Napoli fan was awarded €1500 by an Italian court which ruled in August 2008 that banners describing Naples as the 'sewer of Italy' displayed at the San Siro by Inter Milan fans had caused him 'existential damage'.

291. TWIN STRIKERS

When Ruud van Nistelrooy and Patrick Kluivert were playing up front for Holland in the late 1990s they had more than ability in common – both were born on July 1, 1976.

Not only were these two joined by their birthdays but so, in the same side, were keeper Edwin van der Saar and Phillip Cocu, who were both born on October 29, 1970.

The best chance of an English club boasting genuine twin strikers of that nature might be if Peter Crouch and Dimitar Berbatov ever end up in the same side, as both were born on January 30, 1981.

292. UNSIXCESSFUL

It didn't look good for Charlton – they were 5-1 down at home in their December 1957 Division Two game against Bill Shankly-managed Huddersfield, with 28 minutes remaining – and were down to ten men at a time when no subs were permitted.

Nineteen minutes later Charlton were 6-5 up, Johnny Summers having scored five of them.

Four minutes later, Huddersfield, who had future England World Cup-winning full-back Ray Wilson in their side, equalised.

But there was still time for Athletic to gain a famous victory as their forward, Ryan, hit the winner past despairing Town keeper Kennon, who did manage to get a touch on the ball but could not keep it out.

No team at the time of writing has ever scored six league goals and ended up on the losing side.

Shankly was not best pleased – 'He didn't speak to anybody for days afterwards,' recalled Huddersfield's Ken Taylor later.

293. LOOK BEHIND YOU; OH YES THEY ARE CLOGGERS!

Many sides are accused of being over-physical in their approach to the game, but few have ever been lampooned in a pantomime as a result.

Yet, back in 1887 a team from the Lancashire town of Swinton was accused of such tactics in a very public way, as the *Athletic News* paper reported:

'Football plays a prominent part in more than one pantomime. At the Manchester Comedy (theatre) one of the knockabout merchants comes on the stage arranged in a Manchester jersey, and leaning on a crutch. He limps badly, has his right arm in a sling, a shade over one eye, and pieces of black plaster artistically arranged all over his face.

'His entrance is followed by the remark that the performer has been playing in a football match against Swinton.

'The people from that peaceful village say that the whole thing is a gross caricature, and talk about an action for libel, but when I was there on Friday night some of the audience laughed in a wickedly malicious manner.'

294. BARELY WORTH IT

The excitement of taking a 1-2 lead at Torquay proved too much for one Blackpool fan who, during the August 2000 match, decided to streak in celebration, delaying the match for four minutes.

During the time added on for his ill-advised strip show, Torquay rallied to score twice and win the game 3-2.

295. DEAD TO THE WORLD

England striker Kevin Phillips was not displaying necrophiliac tendencies when he slept with the dead.

The much-travelled star began his career with non-league Baldock Town, whose boss Gary Roberts recalled the aftermath of 'a heavy club night at the end of the season', after which a thoroughly refreshed Phillips headed off home with fellow players.

En route an overwhelming urge for a lie down and kip overtook him and he decided to get his head down for a while – realising in the morning, 'when he woke up on top of a dead person', that he had chosen the local cemetery to sleep it off.

296. DEADLY SEATS

Southampton FC were chary of the deadly potential of the seats from their old home ground, the Dell. When they moved to their current home, St Mary's, they were banned from raising funds by selling off the seats to supporters by health and safety laws, because the seats were deemed potentially fatal – to anyone sucking or eating them.

297. HOWZAT!

Portsmouth striker Rory Allen, 25, announced he was quitting the game to join the Army – the 'Barmy Army' of cricket fans who follow the England team around the world.

Pompey's chief executive, Peter Storrie, said of the November 2002 decision: 'I've never heard anything like it.'

298. WELL, I'LL BE BURGERED!

Referee Paul Durkin demanded police protection during the Oldham versus Chelsea FA Cup tie in January 1999 – after being hit by what he described as 'a frankfurter enclosed in a bread bun'.

Match stewards were indignant, insisting that he had actually been on the receiving end of 'a pastry covered sausage roll'.

Bravely, Durkin eventually and heroically continued with the game and avoided any further contact with fast food.

299. WE'LL WALK IT, LADS

New Everton coach Ian Buchan decided to stamp his authority on the side as they travelled to their 1956 fixture against Leeds United.

A fitness fanatic, Buchan had the team coach halted two miles from Elland Road and told his players to walk the rest of the way to the ground. They lost 5-1.

300. FIDDLING ABOUT

Noted violinist Nigel Kennedy demonstrated his love for Aston Villa by having one of his violins, valued at up to £2.3 million, hand painted in claret and blue.

∗ Jack Southworth, an FA Cup winner with Blackburn Rovers in 1890 and 1891, went on to become a professional violinist with the Halle Orchestra.

301. DON'T PANIC!

A substitute for a non-league team in Arnold, Nottinghamshire, was sent off during a game in April 1999 after the linesman complained to the referee that the player was 'repeatedly whistling the *Dad's Army* theme tune' at him.

He was dismissed for 'intimidating an official'.

Stupid boy!

302. FIRM CONCLUSION

'The Old Firm', a phrase describing Celtic and Rangers, made its first appearance in print on April 16, 1904, the day of the Scottish Cup final which was, for the third time in a decade, to be played between the two clubs.

The *Scottish Referee* published a cartoon in which was depicted a man with a sandwich board on which were written the words 'Patronise the Old Firm – Rangers Celtic Ltd'.

Supporters of the two sides were becoming a little suspicious of the number of draws played out between the two clubs when they met in Cup competitions – producing lucrative turnover for them.

Speculation of this nature reached a new high when in 1909 the pair met again in the final and drew 2-2, before finishing 1–1 in the replay. The crowd demanded extra-time to avoid another expensive replay, and a pitch invasion ensued that led to a full-scale riot, the turnstiles being torched while the police and fire brigade became embroiled in the situation with 5,000 supporters.

The Cup was abandoned and medals withheld.

303. THROUGH ON AWAY GOALS – AT HOME

The Bahamas progressed in their World Cup qualifier against British Virgin Islands in early 2008 on away goals – even though they had been playing at home.

The CONCACAF first stage tie's first leg finished 1-1 in Nassau – but with the BVI's home stadium ruled unsuitable to stage the second leg under FIFA regulations, the Bahamas also hosted the second leg, which ended in a 2-2 draw, putting the actual home side through on away goals as they were officially the away team on their home ground!

304. BOOKED – FOR BEING ABUSED

Racially abused by a home fan during a French league game at Metz during the 2007-08 season, Valenciennes' Moroccan defender Abdeslam Ouaddou was so disgusted that he walked off the pitch – and was promptly booked for dissent.

Metz later had a point docked and were ordered to play behind closed doors.

305. BOUNCED CZECH

Stanislav Griga was sent off for being a Czech during a March 1991 game between his club Feyenoord and Willem II in the Dutch league.

When Feyenoord brought on former Norwich player Mark Farrington in the 67th minute they inadvertently broke a Dutch FA rule that only two non-national players could play for a club at any one time, as they also had a Hungarian in their ranks.

When the referee's attention was drawn to the situation he promptly sent Griga off, but would not allow Feyenoord to replace him with another sub – and they lost 1-0.

306. LOAN DANGER

Andy McCombie, Sunderland and Scotland right-back and a key member of his club's 1903 title-winning side, was, during that year, given £100 by club chairman Sinclair Todd to enable him to launch a new business.

McCombie, 25, was then granted a benefit match – but after it was played Todd demanded the £100 back.

McCombie declared that it had been a gift and he had no intention of returning it. Then, in January 1904, directly as a result of the dispute over the money, he quit to join rivals Newcastle United.

Within a year of his arrival, Newcastle won the league and reached the FA Cup final while Sunderland declined.

Todd resorted to the courts to demand his cash back and won the case. But it was to prove a pyrrhic victory, as the FA intervened to ask why the money was paid in the first place. They held an inquiry, which exonerated McCombie but resulted in a £250 fine for the club and, far worse, a two-and-a-half-year suspension for six directors, including Todd and a three-month suspension for manager Alex Mackie.

307. NAME OF TWO HALVES

A Bulgarian fan was determined to demonstrate his support for Manchester United – by changing his name from Marin Levidzhev to Manchester United.

However, the Bulgarian legal system was determined not to let him, on the grounds that support for a football club was not a sufficient reason to justify such a change.

Levidzhev set off on a two-year legal battle to win the right to the name change, and in February 2007 the system relented – a little – enabling him to become known officially as Manchester Levidzhev.

Marin, er, Manchester, declared that he would take the case to a higher court to enable him to go all the way. 'I feel as if I am only at the half-time break. I won't feel right until I get all my name changed to Manchester United. I love the club. It's my whole life and I want my name to reflect that.'

308. 19TH CENTURY BECKS?

David Beckham made great play of the way in which he was helping to popularise 'soccer' in the USA by joining LA Galaxy – but he is far from being the first from the home of football to try to spread the word in America.

Way back in 1894 four Manchester City players – Calvey, Ferguson, Little and Wallace accepted down payments of £10 each and the promise of up to £5 per week thereafter from an American agent to join Baltimore, one of the clubs involved in a new Professional League in the States, designed to attract the interest of spectators during the baseball close season.

The players going over from England were also to act as coaches for baseball players themselves to see whether they could adapt to football.

The four, plus Sheffield United's Davies sailed on October 3, 1984 on board

The Teutonic but found they had sailed into a storm on arrival, as the US authorities were considering the legality of their new employment as 'aliens' to the country.

When their agent declared he had brought the players over to visit relatives they realised the writing was on the wall, and when the league folded even before it had kicked off they made their way back to England – albeit returning as below-decks passengers rather than enjoying the saloon-class travel of their outward voyage.

On their return they discovered they had been suspended by the FA.

309. YOU BET CHARLIE MET TRAGIC END

Newcastle keeper Charlie Watts in the early 20th century was something of a gambling man – he would discuss racing results with spectators during matches – and after retiring in 1906 he earned a living by becoming a professional racing tipster.

But he met a tragic end in 1924 when he took his own life by cutting his throat.

310. FOGGED OFF

Newcastle skipper Hughie Gallacher was far from pleased with referee Mr A E Fogg who twice denied him what he believed were cast-iron penalties in a 3-2 defeat by Huddersfield in a 1927 New Year's Eve match.

Fogg told the protesting Gallacher: 'I'm reporting you.'

After the game Gallacher continued the discussion, telling the ref 'Fogg is your name and you've been in a fog all day'.

Finally calming down, Gallacher decided to apologise to the referee, so walked into his changing room – only to find him bending over the steaming bath.

He pushed Fogg straight in.

Gallacher was suspended for two months.

311. ROLLED OUT

With German side Gladbach a goal up in their 1970-71 European Cup first leg game, keeper Wolfgang Kleff decided to remove a roll of toilet paper, thrown on to the pitch from the crowd, from his penalty area.

While he was doing so, Everton's Howard Kendall looked up and saw the distracted custodian, and equalised from distance.

Everton eventually won the tie on a penalty shoot-out.

312. HOW 14-YEAR-OLD KNOCKED SPAIN OUT OF WORLD CUP

Spain had to overcome then little known Turkey in a two-leg game to reach the finals of the 1954 World Cup, but after winning the first leg 4-1 and losing the second 0-1 they had to meet again in a play-off – this was in the days before away goals counted double.

The play-off was scheduled for three days later in Rome. Ten minutes before kick-off a FIFA official strode into the Spaniards' dressing room and showed them a document that forbade them to field their star player, Hungarian-born Kubala, on the grounds that his previous appearances for Hungary ruled him out.

Disconcerted by this intervention, Spain played poorly and only managed a 2-2 draw with a late equaliser.

This meant that the names of Spain and Turkey would have to be drawn from a silver tankard to see who went through. A blindfolded 14-year-old Italian boy called, ironically enough, Franco, duly pulled out Turkey's name.

The Spaniards' mood was not remotely improved the next day when FIFA denied point blank having sent anyone into the Spanish dressing room before the play-off game and confirmed that Kubala had been perfectly qualified to play.

313. WHAT A DICK

Garrincha, legendary Brazilian player of the 1950s and '60s, was known not only for his bizarrely curved legs, but also for the reported size of a different part of his anatomy.

When his biographer, Ruy Castro, went into print declaring that a terrace song which suggested Garrincha, from the town of Pau Grande, was also the owner of a 'pau grande' or , in slang terms, 'big d**k' that was 25cm long, he was promptly sued for libel.

However, the judge hearing the case found in Castro's favour: 'It should be noted that it is a matter of pride, at least in this country, to have a large member.'

Garrincha's appendage may or may not have been larger than average. That it was in full working order is not in doubt – his offspring numbered into double figures.

314. SURELY NOT!!

It is as though we had just discovered that the Queen has bodily functions, or that Sir Bobby Charlton had once trashed a dressing room.

Franz Beckenbauer, aka 'Der Kaiser', perhaps the greatest, certainly the most respected of German players, was once fined DM1,000 because he 'provoked the crowd' after a December 1968 match for his club Bayern Munich away to Hanover.

After the game, in which Bayern's Gerd Muller had been sent off, Beckenbauer's teammate Sepp Maier was attacked by a fan with an umbrella – and responded by punching the assailant to the ground.

As Beckenbauer left the pitch, he pretended to urinate at Hanover supporters!

There's more – in 1963 Beckenbauer impregnated his girlfriend, when he was just 18, but refused to marry her, whereupon he was banned from the national youth team!

He was later pardoned, on condition that he shared a double room – with coach Dettmar Cramer.

315. WILL HE SCHU UP?

Michael Schumacher, former F1 World Champion, was invited by San Marino-based club Murata to play for them in their 2008/9 Champions League qualifying round match. He declined the offer.

316. I CANNY LAD SEE CLEARLY NOW

Newcastle's defeat in the 1908 FA Cup final by Wolves had an unexpectedly positive result for motorists.

For Newcastle fan Gladstone Adams, from South Shields, drove to and from the match, encountering hail on the return trip, which made it difficult to see where he was going.

The adaptable Adams rigged up a mechanical contrivance to clear the hail from his windscreen. Once at home, he refined his idea into the first windscreen wipers.

317. JAW, JAW

Colchester United's Bobby Blackwood broke his jaw after colliding with QPR striker Les Allen during their Division Three match in August 1966.

Back in action when the return game took place in December the same year, the half-back broke his jaw after colliding with QPR striker Les Allen.

318. WEDDING DAY BILLS

Both Bill Poyntz, for Leeds United against Leicester City on February 20, 1922, and Bill Holmes for Southport against Carlisle United on October 30, 1954,scored hat-tricks in Football League matches – on their wedding day.

One assumes they also scored later the same day.

319. BLAZING MAD

After nine-year-old goalkeeper Natasha Dennis turned in a great performance for her side Lewisville Blaze during a 1990 match in America, parents from the opposing side demanded that she undergo an impromptu 'sex test'.

'The harassment extended to asking her to go to the bathroom with a designated 'objective' parent who would verify her sex,' it was reported. *Los Angeles Times* writer Gary Libman said: 'The goalie was a girl but parents wanted proof. Others wondered why the issue was even raised.'

320. TRAUMATIC TRUTH

England fan Paul Hucker, 34, from Ipswich was so concerned that if England were knocked out of the 2006 World Cup finals in the early stages he would suffer psychological trauma, that he insured himself to receive £1 million if it happened, respected news agency the Press Association reported in May, before the tournament got under way.

If England performed badly and he could provide medical evidence that he had suffered severe medical trauma then Hucker, who had paid a premium of £100, would be in line for the payout from web-based insurance company britishinsurance.com, added the PA story, which was widely covered in the media worldwide. 'I find when it goes to penalty shoot-outs it gets very difficult, and I wanted to insure myself against psychological trauma,' Hucker was reported as saying.

In February 2008, the *UK Press Gazette*, a trade paper for journalists, carried a story claiming that the Hucker-britishinsurance.com yarn was 'not exactly reliable'. It was 'a neat little tale designed to promote an insurance company – the story was not only unreliable, it was also old. Hucker had appeared in exactly the same story in the run up to the previous World Cup in Japan in 2002'.

Hucker, said the Gazette, was a marketing director who 'specialises in promoting web-based companies'.

321. DON'T BOTHER ABOUT THE TIP, GUV!

Liverpool's Martin Skrtel jumped into a cab and asked to be taken home, in March 2008, only to be thrown out of the vehicle by the driver, who told the Slovak centre-back that he was an Everton fan. 'When he realised he was dealing with a Liverpool player he showed me the door,' said Skrtel.

322. VEIN HOPE

'It could give them varicose veins,' explained the chief of the Soviet Sports Federation, Dr Natalya Grayevskaya, in September 1972 as she justified the Ministry of Health's ban on women's football.

She added: 'And worse, it could damage the functioning of the sexual organs. A woman's pelvis is not just a firm support for the spine and lower limbs – a hard ball kicked there could damage organs protecting the pelvic ring.'

Mind you, some 50 years earlier, British football authorities had been little less enlightened when in 1921 they clamped down on ladies football on the spurious grounds that it was an unsuitable game for females and that funds from some of the well-attended games which were being staged 'were being misappropriated'.

The FA barred women from playing on affiliated pitches and banned registered referees from officiating at the games.

Teams had been playing very popular charity fund-raising games on professional Football League teams' grounds after the First World War.

Among the most popular teams was the Dick, Kerr Ladies (almost immediately dubbed the 'Dickless Kerrs' according to historian of the ladies' game, Jean Williams), a factory team from Preston who were playing in front of crowds of up to 35,000. On Boxing Day 1920, at Goodison Park, Dick, Kerr and St Helens attracted a reported 55,000, raising more than £3,000 for former servicemen.

★ When TV presenter Hughie Green's reputation was savaged in a 2008 BBC drama, it was not revealed that in 1970 he had sponsored and promoted a women's football tournament – matches taking place at various Butlin's holiday camps – after being challenged to do so by a female contestant on his enormously popular talent show, 'Opportunity Knocks!'

323. THAT'S US BULGARED, THEN

CSKA Sofia, perhaps the most famous of Bulgarian clubs, ceased to exist for three years when the Committee of the Bulgarian Communist Party disbanded them and their Bulgarian Cup final opponents, Levski Spartak, in June 1985 after the match between the two produced a number of punch-ups on the pitch and attacks on the referee.

CSKA won the game but the Communist Party was not impressed and renamed CSKA 'Sredets' and Levski 'Vitosha', under which names the clubs played until being reinstated in 1988.

However, neither of them was allowed in the European Cup and their place was taken instead by Trakia Ploivdiv, who had finished third to the pair in the league – and they crashed out to IFK Gothenburg in round one.

324. THERE'S GRATITUDE FOR YOU!

When Russian tanks rolled into Czechoslovakia in August 1968 to crush its liberal regime, led by Alexander Dubcek, Celtic made a noble gesture by withdrawing from their European Cup first round tie with Ferencvaros of Hungary, one of the Warsaw Pact bloc clubs.

Some other clubs threatened to join them, so UEFA scrapped the draw, but re-drew it, segregating Western and Eastern bloc clubs, thus creating more problems and resulting in the withdrawal of eastern European clubs.

However, despite all the fuss on their behalf, the Czech club Spartak Trnava remained in the event, and reached the semi-final – further than the reinstated Celtic managed.

325. NOT SO BRAVO FOR RIO

When Portsmouth scored the penalty that knocked Manchester United out of the FA Cup quarter-finals in March 2008 in front of their own fans, Rio Ferdinand was in goal for the home side.

The England player hadn't started in that position, of course. The defender found himself between the sticks after Edwin van der Saar had started there, only to suffer an injury that saw him replaced by Tomas Kuszczak, who was then red-carded as he conceded the penalty that enabled Portsmouth boss Harry Redknapp to mastermind an FA Cup elimination of United for the third time.

Asked after the game about the fact that it was Portsmouth's first win at Old Trafford for 51 years, Harry observed: 'We won at Newcastle recently and they told me we hadn't won there for 200 years.'

326. THIRTY PIECES OF SILVER SPARKED NORTH-EAST RIVALRY

Sunderland beat local rivals Middlesbrough 4-2 in the 1887-88 FA Cup after a 2-2 draw in their first game.

But their progress into the last 16 was halted when they were thrown out of the competition after the FA decided that they had breached the competition's rules, which specified that any professionals must have been born locally or have lived within six miles of the club for the previous two years.

Sunderland's books listed 'a payment of 30 shillings' to Hastings, Monaghan and Richardson for train fares from Dumfries in Scotland to Sunderland. They were Scots, clearly not living locally.

Sunderland were outraged – even more so when they discovered that the whistle had been blown on them by Middlesbrough.

The incident still rankles.

327. CUTTING REMARKS

BBC journalist John Barnes had no reason to believe that his interview with respected Dundee United chairman Jim McLean after their 4-0 defeat by Hearts during the 2000 season would be anything other than routine.

But when Barnes asked McLean about the future of United boss Alex Smith, the chairman initially swore and refused to answer the question.

As they moved off-camera McLean reportedly struck Barnes on the face with his fist, leaving the reporter bleeding from a cut lip and needing treatment from the club doctor.

Less than an hour later, McLean resigned after seven years as chairman. He later made a public apology.

328. NEVER SHORT OF PLAYERS

Giants of the North are a Brazilian football team consisting entirely of dwarfs.

Managed by professional coach Carlos Lucena, the team claimed to be the first of their type in April 2008 when boasting players ranging from 3ft 7in tall to their tallest player, at 4ft 7in, who plays in goal.

Playing 50-minute matches, usually against youth teams in northern Brazil, the all-aged side was set up to integrate dwarfs into society and to prevent the increase of 'sizeism' in Brazilian society. Allegedly.

329. HE'S FREE TO PLAY

Gordon Bartlett, manager of Stuart Pearce and Vinnie Jones's former team, Wealdstone, of the Ryman Premier League, believed he had solved his defensive crisis when he managed to persuade promising American youngster Rhett Bernstein to sign on in April 2008.

Gordon was set to slot the student into his back four for the game at Maidstone United after gaining international clearance for him.

However, he had to scrap the plans when he discovered that Bernstein could only play if the crowd was allowed in for free!

'The problem was his visa,' explained Bartlett. 'If he had had a full student visa or work permit, it would have been okay, but he only had a short-term visa which means we couldn't play him in front of anyone paying to get in – or pay him either.

'We could hardly blame Maidstone for not wanting to allow spectators in for free!'

330. SIR ALEX PACKS IT IN

Fans wondered whether Sir Alex Ferguson might have been taken ill or perhaps was on the verge of retirement when he mysteriously failed to turn up at either of the two Manchester United friendlies being played in early August 2007 against Dunfermline and Glentoran.

The long-serving Old Trafford supremo was, in fact, helping wife Cathy to pack, prior to the pair moving home.

'I told her that I had a match tonight,' he said. 'But she wasn't having any of it. She said I had to help her.'

331. A BIT WEEK

Welsh club, Abergavenny Thursdays, announced proudly in their club details – 'Midweek fixtures normally played on Wednesdays'.

Thus named because they originally played only on the town's half day closing afternoon, the former Welsh League champions are the only other British side, apart from Sheffield Wednesday, to incorporate a day of the week in their name.

Various players have done so – such as Nigerian World Cup 1998 star, Sunday Oliseh, and maverick Reading hero, Robin Friday, immortalized in the book *The Greatest Football Player You Never Saw*.

332. NO-ONE LIKES US – WE'RE UNDER THE WEATHER

Millwall attracted a unique sponsorship deal for the 1997-98 season – when they wore kit sporting the slogan 'The Weather In Norwegian' after doing a deal with cable TV channel Live TV – whose glamorous weather girl, Norwegian Anne Marie Foss, became the club mascot as part of the arrangement.

∗ When Scotland played Norway in a 1998 World Cup game their fans taunted the opposition with the inventive chant: 'Sing when you're whaling, you only sing when you're whaling'!

333. THREE-ALL

Three-sided football is a variation of football with three teams instead of the usual two.

It was devised by the Danish 'situationist' Asger Jorn to explain his notion of trioletics, his refinement on the Marxian concept of dialetics, as well as to disrupt the everyday idea of football. It is played on a hexagonal pitch.

Unlike in conventional football, where the winner is determined by the highest scoring of the two teams, no score is kept of the goals which a team scores, but conversely a count is taken of the number of goals conceded and the winning team is that which concedes the least number of goals.

The game purports to 'deconstruct the confrontational and bi-polar nature of conventional football as an analogy of class struggle in which the referee stands as a signifier of the state and media apparatus, posturing as a neutral arbitrator in the political process of ongoing class struggle'.

The first known game played was organised by the London Psychogeographical Association at the Glasgow Anarchist Summer School in 1993.

334. PAPE-AL TURNABOUT

Albert Pape arrived at Old Trafford with his Clapton Orient teammates for their Second Division fixture against Manchester United on February 7, 1925.

An hour before kick-off it was announced that Pape, who had scored 11 goals in 24 appearances for Orient, had signed for United, for whom he turned out – and scored in the 4-2 home win.

335. SPEEDY DEPARTURE

When Gary Speed left Everton for Newcastle in 1998 he cited among the reasons for his departure the fact that he had been unable to secure a complimentary ticket for an FA Cup tie, and that the food on the Everton team coach had allegedly not been hot enough for his liking.

336. CARR ACCIDENT

England took to the field for the March 1875 international against Scotland with the players, who hailed from seven different clubs, having 'adopted various costumes' according to a contemporary report.

But there was another unusual element to their line-up – they started with only ten men against the Scots , who were wearing 'blue jerseys and knickerbockers'.

England goalkeeper Billy Carr of Sheffield had arrived late, and didn't make it on to the pitch until a 'few' minutes after kick-off – but his teammates had managed to keep the score goalless.

The game, at Kennington Oval cricket ground, ended in a 2-2 draw.

337. GETTING SHIRTY

The hard-up Albanian FA banned players from swapping shirts after their game against Spain in September 1993, as they could not afford replacements.

338. DYEING TO PLAY

Bradford City player Jamie Lawrence spent the 1999-2000 Premiership season varying the colour of his hair for matches – turning out with his crowning glory purple, blonde, scarlet and bright green among other colours.

339. URINE TROUBLE

Sent off for swearing, Darren Painter took revenge on the referee – by telling his stepsons to urinate in his shoes.

29-year-old Painter, from Swindon, sent off for Buckland FC in the Berkshire League, was kicked out of the club and had his registration cancelled by the league in November 1999.

340. PEARCED OFF

Housewife Diane Anderson was so obsessed with Stuart Pearce that whenever she read that he was injured she administered Tiger Balm ointment to a lifesize cut-out of the player.

The 53-year-old civil servant from Deeping St James, Lincolnshire, featured in a 1998 Channel 4 show in which she revealed that she also talked to her Pearce cut-out and had even taken 'him' with her to parties. 'I love his thighs,' she explained.

Husband John, a tolerant type, commented: 'I draw the line at one thing – I won't let 'him' into bed.'

★ Stuart Pearce was announced as the winner of the PFA Fair Play award in
  August 1991 – but was then sent off for swearing while playing on the
  same day.

341. TAKE NOTICE

Opponents turning up for matches against the Ford Open Prison side during the 1999-2000 season may have been a little surprised to see the dressing-room notice warning them to 'Beware of Thieves'.

342. HOW TO HAMMER THE REST

'When training, Oxo is the only beverage used by our team and all speak of the supreme strength and power of endurance which they have derived from its use,' declared West Ham's secretary/manager Syd King in a testimonial for the product during the 1904-05 season.

343. SHORTS STORM

FIFA president Sepp Blatter revealed his masterplan for making women's football more popular during a January 2004 interview with a Swiss newspaper: 'Let the women play in more feminine clothes like they do in volleyball. They could, for example, have tighter shorts. They already have some different rules to men – such as playing with a lighter ball.'

The comments were not generally well received. 'We don't use a lighter ball,' said England and Charlton goalkeeper Pauline Cop, adding that the comments were 'typical of a bloke. To say we should play football in hotpants is plain ridiculous.' Ridiculous, indeed, and not even Blatter actually said that!

'Ten years ago we did play in tighter shorts,' pointed out Fulham manager Marieanne Spacey. 'Nobody paid attention then.'

344. YES! WE'VE WON THE, ER, NOTHING!

Nuremberg and Hamburg were locked at 2-2 after 90 minutes of the 1922 German championship final. So, as was the custom back then, the game would continue until the deadlock was broken.

After three hours and ten minutes with players now staggering around, referee

Dr Peco Bauwens decided that the light had deteriorated so badly that he called off the ordeal.

The replay also went into extra-time, but when Nuremberg went down to seven players because of sendings off and injuries Bauwens again called the game off.

Eventually, the football authorities decreed that Hamburg should be 'theoretically' the winners – but that the club should also renounce the trophy.

345. MR LOOPHOLE, FOOTBALL'S DRIVING FORCE?

Celebrity lawyer Nick Freeman became known as 'Mr Loophole' after helping a number of high-profile football figures avoid prosecution for alleged motoring offences.

In 1999 Freeman successfully argued that Sir Alex Ferguson was driving on the hard shoulder of a motorway because he needed to get to a lavatory.

David Beckham was found not guilty of a speeding charge when Freeman argued 'duress of circumstance' – that he was being chased by paparazzi at the time.

Dwight Yorke was acquitted of a driving ban when Freeman argued that the police had incorrectly used a speed gun.

Wayne Rooney was acquitted of charges of driving without insurance when Freeman had them overturned due to 'administrative errors'.

346. SICK AS A BLUE-NOSE

When a Rangers fan who never missed a game when they were on the TV went missing in autumn 2005 a major search was launched by the 12-year-old's guardian, Liz Fagan.

He had vanished from his home in Tooting, south London but Liz was optimistic that his strong Scottish accent would lead to him being found very quickly.

Sadly, at the time of writing, no-one had discovered the African grey parrot!

347. FOR HEAVEN'S SAKE

Red cards were issued for taking the name of the Lord in vain and blue cards were issued for lesser offences, which resulted in a spell in the sin bin when a tournament was launched in 2006 for teams of priests.

The Clericus Cup involved 16 teams, and more than 200 clergymen from over 50 countries. No games were played on Sundays and, to encourage older people to play, they were 30 minutes each way.

The opening game featured a team called Mater Ecclesiae, whose keeper was called Jesus.

The tournament was organised by the Italian Sporting Centre, which promotes Christian activity through sport. In the final in May 2007 there were arguments over diving and a flourishing of blue cards as the game between the Pontifical Lateran University and Redemptoris Mater College was decided in favour of the latter thanks to a hotly disputed penalty.

348. PLUS ÇA CHANGE

'Europe has too slavishly followed the cult of personality. Players are known, not for their ability, but by their price tag and earnings. The blame for this preoccupation with money must be shared by players, directors, managers, press, radio, television and the public.

'All have allowed, and at times encouraged, the size of the transfer fee and the wage packet to become the status symbol of professional footballers, while the Latin Americans and the Communists have made ball control, shooting and tactics the criteria by which they judge their players.

In Italy, Spain and England in particular, over-publicized stars are bought for vast sums, used for a season or two, then replaced by new, expensive names. That money should be spent on finding and developing talent for employment over an extended period.'

The giveaway is that word 'Communist' – the only thing that might mitigate against this critique of the state of football having been written within the last few months.

Journalist Donald Saunders wrote this passage in his book *World Cup 1962*.

349. EASY AS PIE MISTAKE

Imre Varadi was so overcome with joy at scoring for Everton against deadly rivals Liverpool that he raced towards the Toffees' fans to celebrate – only to find himself confronting ranks of Liverpool supporters.

'One of them threw a pie straight in his face,' recalled Steve McMahon, asked for the funniest memory of his career.

350. BERNIE'S BUM DEAL

'If Middlesbrough beat Manchester United I'll bare my backside in Binns' window,' vowed former Boro favourite – 119 league goals in 297 games – Bernie Slaven to listeners of his Century FM radio show.

Inevitably, Boro won 3-2 at the Riverside, so the Slaven posterior was duly unveiled in the department store's window.

'When I got down there, there were 3,000 people waiting to see my bum,' he remembered.

351. ROBBERTO CARLOS

The precise details are a little difficult to unravel but the basic fact seems true enough – while conducting a live media interview in June 2005 in his native Brazil, Real Madrid star Roberto Carlos was involved in a gunpoint robbery.

Differing reports of the incident, most of which position him at a stop-light, r stuck in traffic in Belo Horizonte, have him either in the front or back of his, or a journalist's motor; either being interviewed by camera for TV, or talking on a mobile to a radio station. His girlfriend/bodyguard are either in the car with him or not, and there were one or two gunman/men who arrived on foot or on a motorcycle. Either Carlos and/or the journalist were robbed.

Carlos is reported as commenting: 'They just robbed my car. That's never happened to me before. What a scare.'

352. SOMERS-OUCH

Celestine Babayaro was delighted with his pre-season friendly goal for Chelsea against Stevenage Borough in 1997, celebrating it with a spectacular backward somersault – as a result of which he broke his leg.

353. WHAT'S THAT FOUR, REF?

I was in the crowd at Kenilworth Road when Luton beat Bradford City 4-0 in a League One game in November 2004 and, like most spectators, was astonished when ref Joe Ross booked City's Dean Windass, for the second time that afternoon, after the final whistle and brandished the red card at him. He also held up four fingers to the burly striker in what appeared to be a reference to the score.

Aftewards, it emerged that Ross was being accused of taunting Windass and other players by repeating to them 'four nil, four nil'.

Unsurprisingly, Windass appealed against his sending off, and the second card was eventually rescinded.

Bradford also demanded that Ross should not ref any more of their games.

354. BRANN NEW APOLOGY

Perhaps overcome by the emotion of winning their first title in 44 years, Norwegian champions Brann launched a book about the famous season with the slogan: 'Do you want to read about pig farmers or gays – or PROPER MEN?'

There were objections. Not, apparently, from the pig farmers.

'We apologise. We respect everyone, whatever sort of sex they like,' said Brann director Bjorn Dahl.

355. CURRYING FAVOUR

Fans watching England take on Trinidad & Tobago ordered a takeaway curry to be delivered at the end of the match in Germany – from their favourite curry house in Bath!

Members of the Opposite Worlds dance troupe had the curry sent to their hotel in Munich – at a cost of £1,600 – from Bombay Nights in Bath, whose manager Abdul Nasir, 32, flew out with the meal which included chicken, mirchi fish, lamb karahi, king prawns together with rices, naan breads and starters.

'We thought it was a wind-up until we received a deposit and knew it was genuine,' said Nasir.

356. NOT HERE, MATE!

Cameroon Premier League side Bamboutos suffered a two-division relegation after their match-winning tactics against Federal proved a little too blatant.

The Times reported in October 2007: 'A referee saw Koss Roger, their captain, handing an envelope of cash to Nkouna Rim, captain of Federal, on the pitch. Minutes later, Rim let Roger in to score the decider in his team's 3-2 win.'

357. WE'RE CROSS: FANS

Macedonian side Vardar Skopje were left in no doubt as to the feelings of the fans who marked their elimination from the UEFA Cup by a side from Cyprus in the early stages of the 2007-08 season by digging a grave overnight in the middle of the stadium and leaving on it a cross, bearing the message: 'RIP 2007 Uprava (management)'.

Coach Dragi Kanatlarovski was duly fired.

358. CHILLED-OUT HORSE

It is not uncommon for racehorses to be named after footballing heroes – with current stars like Schevchenko, Ryan Giggs, Van Nistelrooy, Solskjaer, John Terry and Tevez being so honoured, but Cambridge United's striker Dan Chillingworth was a surprise addition to the equine footballing ranks in September 2007.

An Indian Ridge colt trained by James Fanshawe was given the name 'Chillingworth' by Fanshawe's football-mad ten year old son Tom – who had become a great fan of the player when he met him at a Cambridge open day.

359. SAVAGE DECISION

Robbie Savage has been accused of getting other players sent off or booked before – but the combative Wales midfielder was the unwitting reason for the dismissal of airline pilot Captain Pablo Mason during the 2007-08 season.

Blackburn were travelling home from a game in Finland when the pilot permitted Savage, a nervous flyer, to visit the flight deck – in strict contravention of anti-terrorism security rules, resulting in his subsequent sacking by MyTravel Airways.

360. BIT OF BROTH-ER

Italian fourth division side Trentino 1921 came in for criticism in October 2007 over the £7,000 sponsorship deal they had arranged – with an Austrian brothel.

361. WHO WAS THAT MASKED MAN?

Fulham's Argentinian striker Facundo Sava celebrated his two-goal haul for Fulham against Liverpool on November 23, 2002 in flamboyant style, demonstrating where his nickname of 'Zorro' had come from as he whipped out and donned a black and white mask.

362. BALD STATEMENT

Chelsea delayed a 1998 press conference because '[manager] Mr Vialli is shaving his head'.

363. CHIEFLY FORGOTTEN

Chart-topping band the Kaiser Chiefs share their name with, and took it from, the top South African football club Kaizer Chiefs, albeit the spelling is one letter different.

Band front man Ricky Wilson explained: 'When we were looking for a name, we went through loads of names because you've always got one band member that's not gonna be happy with it, you know. Kaiser Chiefs was the first thing suggested to us that we all kind of thought was all right. And then we found out that the Kaiser Chiefs are a soccer team for South Africa. We didn't know it at the time. And also, one of their players now plays for Leeds United, and we're from Leeds, so we thought, well ...'

But I wonder how many of the band's fans are aware of the tragic consequences on January 13, 1991, when a controversial penalty was awarded during the club's match at the Ernest Oppenheimer Stadium in Western Transvaal, against Orlando Pirates.

A crowd disturbance broke out, as a result of which 40 fans died and 50 more were injured.

364. WATER JOKE

Haydock, the visitors to Stockport County on January 6, 1900, were not happy that they were 5-1 down after 65 minutes – but were even less enamoured that the ref refused to heed their pleas that the torrential downpour in which the match was being played had made the playing surface, well, unfit for purpose.

The ref waved their objections aside and told them to get on with it. County did and during the next 15 minutes hammered another four goals. However, as the goals were raining in, Haydock players were walking off in protest and, with ten minutes remaining, the score was 9-1 to Stockport, but Haydock had just five men left on the pitch.

Now the ref abandoned the game.

After an enquiry, the result was allowed to stand.

Sixty-two years later in March 1962, County figured in another bizarre abandonment when winger Gene Wilson was sent off for arguing with the ref in a reserve match against Manchester City. Wilson refused to depart and was warned by the irate arbiter that if he did not leave within the next ten seconds the game would be called off.

He didn't. It was. Wilson was sacked.

365. LIONISED

Hadjuk Split striker Maris Verpakovskis was surprised to find on returning from a 2007-08 mid-season break in Sierra Leone that he was accused of being dead.

According to a number of Croat papers, that is, which had reported that the Latvian had been killed in an attack by lions while on his holiday.

366. SIREN CALL

AFC Sudbury of the Ridgeons League unleashed a secret weapon on opposing teams during the 2008-09 season – an air-raid siren.

Sudbury supporter Richard Instance spotted the siren being auctioned on the eBay website and snapped it up for £250. He then handed it over to club programme editor Chris Rixon.

Rixon and fellow fans take the siren to matches – 'It's genuine World War Two, and even came in a crate with War Department stencilled on it. Since then it has followed us everywhere and always causes a stir wherever we go. However, we do limit its use to corners, free-kicks near the area and, of course, when we score,' Rixon said.

Writing about the effect of the siren on other teams, Stuart Hammonds of Ware, from the same division, commented: 'Defending a free-kick I couldn't hear a thing our keeper James Hoad was shouting at us. I remember thinking, 'Bloody Hell, has World War Three broken out?'

367. BARE-FACED CHEEK

Bill Norman, Hartlepool manager from 1927-31, refused to allow training to be cancelled when the club's pitch was covered in snow. Instead, he 'showed them what could be done by taking off all his clothes and rolling in the snow'.

368. BOOZE SORRY NOW?

The first recorded example of the demon drink getting the better of a star footballer came in 1898, when Scotland's centre-half Jamie Cowan, of Aston Villa, turned in a bizarre performance against England at Parkhead as the Scots went down 3-1.

Failing to make tackles and going on a series of eccentric and pointless dribbles with the ball, Cowan was picked on by the crowd, and several of his teammates, for the defeat.

The Scottish FA instigated an enquiry into his performance during which he was directly accused of being under the influence – and although not officially censured, the incident curtailed his Scotland career.

★ Strict teetotaller and Liverpool legend Billy Liddell, who won 28 Scottish caps, refused point blank to take even a ritual sip of champagne from the trophy when he helped Liverpool to the 1947 championship.

So, when he broke the club record of 429 league games, the club naturally made a presentation to him – 'a cocktail cabinet loaded with all kinds of liquor'.

369. BOTTLING IT

Drawn against Southampton St Mary's in the FA Cup of 1894, Reading were keen to play their forward Jimmy Stewart, a private in the King's Own Regiment, who just happened to be held in detention in the guardroom for a breach of discipline.

Reading secretary Horace Walker thought laterally, and bribed Stewart's guards with bottles of Scotch, securing permission for him to play in the match.

It was doubles all round as Stewart notched the winning goal before returning to complete his jankers.

370. WHAT TOOK HIM SO LONG?

Vinnie Jones, positively revelling in the title 'legendary hardman', exceeded even his own lofty standards on February 15, 1992 when he was booked within THREE seconds of kick-off at Stamford Bridge for a two-footed tackle on Sheffield United's Dane Whitehouse.

This smashed not only Whitehouse, but also Vinnie's record for his fastest ever booking – which had previously stood at a lengthy five seconds, almost twice as long as the new one.

★ Details of who seem to be lost in the mists of time, but it is recorded that on April 8, 1986, ref David Axcell booked a player after two seconds.

371. SKULL-DUGGERY?

Hackney-based club Black Rovers, formed in the 1860s, must have had a considerable psychological advantage over their opponents as soon as they ran on to the pitch wearing their black jerseys emblazoned with a white skull and crossbones motif on the breast.

372. GOLDEN BOY TARNISHED

The 1991 Derby match between Uruguay's two biggest teams, Penarol and Nacional, was in full swing when Nacional's star striker and Panamanian international, Dely Valdez, and Penarol defender Goncalves battled for the ball as a corner was being taken.

Valdez, a colourful, flamboyant player, was widely known for his love of 'bling' and fashion jewellery, and as the ball came over from the corner, Goncalves was all over Valdez, and the TV cameras spotted him ripping a gold chain from the striker's neck and hiding it down one of his socks.

Nobody in the stadium had noticed in the heat of battle but after the game police, who had been alerted by the TV people, were waiting to arrest Goncalves with Valdez in close proximity demanding to know where his chain was.

Charges were later dropped after Goncalves confessed and handed back the chain, commenting: 'I don't know what I was thinking.'

Future matches between the two clubs became known as the 'Golden chain derby'.

373. CREAM OF THE CROP

Manchester United froze out the opposition when they signed Stockport County wing half Hughie McLennan in 1927.

The transfer fee was three freezers of ice-cream – subsequently sold to raise funds at the club bazaar.

374. YOU PLAY FOR WHICH CLUB?

There have been a number of clubs whose names players may have not been over-keen to admit to, such as local Norfolk side Norwich Whifflers, while a club called Remnants graced the FA Cup from 1877 until 1882.

And Wankie, a Premier League club from Zimbabwe, were always unlikely to attract too many British recruits.

Ugandan side Mbale Dairy Heroes have probably always milked their successes among the cream of the country's clubs, while you've got to love the aptly named Swaziland club who were relegated from the Castle Brewery Premier League in 2000, going by the superb name, Eleven Men In Flight. As they then had to play Moneni Pirates, you can see where they were coming from, or perhaps going to.

Seychelles side Sunshine must brighten up their division but it must be the Devil's own job to overcome Reunion National League side Posession.

Nigeria's League One side Shooting Stars belied their name when they were relegated in 1999 – although Liberia's Invincible Eleven have lived up to their name by becoming champions on many occasions.

High crosses into the box are probably the tactic of the day for sides coming up against Ghana's ABC Golden Lager Premier League side Cape Coast Dwarfs – who were relegated in 2000.

Referees serving Botswana's Toyota First Division probably make a note to take a good supply of yellow and red cards with them when they are in charge of Naughty Boys matches. If they ever met up with Jamaican League winners Violent Kickers, it would hardly be a match for faint-hearted players.

375. SCORED – BUT NEVER ON PITCH

A 1937 amateur cup tie produced a unique occurrence when one side's winger scored without ever setting foot on the pitch.

He was late in arriving and the game had started by the time he changed. As he stood on the touchline, awaiting the referee's permission to come on to the pitch, his team attacked and forced a corner.

The referee acknowledged his arrival and waved to him to take the corner kick. He did so, and scored direct.

The incident was recorded by William Lowndes in his 1952 book, *The Story of Football*.

376. CUP WINNERS WEREN'T EVEN IN FINAL

Morpeth Harriers received cup winners' medals without even playing in the final of the 1886 Northumberland Cup.

Shankhouse beat Newcastle West End in the final, having come through the semi-final against the Harriers in extraordinary circumstances.

The two sides had met FIVE times in the semi. In the fourth match a spectator blew a whistle, which caused Morpeth players to stop as Shankhouse attacked and scored, to take a 3-2 lead.

The FA overruled the goal and ordered the fifth meeting.

'This game went on so long,' said a contemporary report, 'that two referees were used. The first left to catch a train. Four hours after kick-off, darkness stopped play with the sides level. The teams had now played for ten and a half hours in total and it was agreed to toss up to see which club should go forward.'

But there was one important condition. Both sides agreed that if the club going forward were to win the final, the trophy should be held jointly.

Shankhouse won the toss – and the final – and Morpeth duly picked up winners' medals.

377. VALE OF TEARS

Vale of Leven reached the 1884 Scottish Cup final, but refused to play in the match when the Scottish FA would not permit them to postpone the date because of player injuries and family bereavements.

They just let Queens Park have the trophy.

378. FACE OFF

The official photographer hired to immortalise the England side before a game at The Oval in 1873 was unsuccessful, said reports at the time, 'because some of the team persisted in pulling faces at the camera'.

The previous year, a photographer approached to do the honours at the first Scotland–England fixture failed to perform his function – because he could not secure an assurance from the Scottish FA that all of the players would purchase copies of his pictures.

Hence, there is no photographic record of the historic match.

379. LOOK INTO MY EYES, LADS.

Hinckley Athletic ran out for their local cup match against Bedworth Town in April 1949 absolutely convinced that they were certain to win.

The players of the Leicestershire side had been hypnotised before kick-off.

They lost 2-1 – but probably still believed they had won!

380. SHIRTY SHILTS

Peter Shilton, who won 125 caps for England, was asked in February 2008 what he most remembered about winning his 100th..

Overlooking the fact that it was a 3-1 1988 Euro Championship defeat by Holland in which Marco van Basten scored a hat-trick, Shilton preferred to dwell on the 'awful' keeper's shirt he was forced to wear – 'green and black zig-zags which must have had TV viewers trying to adjust their aerials'.

★ As a youngster Shilton used to hang from the banisters at his parents' home with weights on his feet in order improve his flexibility and stretch his arms.

381. WHAT GOES AROUND ...

With Spurs leading Arsenal 2-0 on aggregate at half-time of the 1987 League Cup semi-final, the club announced details of final tickets over the public address system.

They were eventually knocked out.

Fast forward to 2008 and Spurs are meeting Arsenal again in a second-leg Carling Cup tie for the right to play at Wembley Stadium in the final.

Arsenal, leading on aggregate, begin talks with Ticketmaster over ticketing arrangements, having decided how to allocate their quota of Cup Final tickets, reported the *Guardian*.

Arsenal were knocked out by Spurs.

382. FOOTBALLER? NO, MATE, I'M A SOLDIER!

Tommy Magee was a surprise selection at inside right for the West Brom side when they faced Derby County at the beginning of the 1919-20 season.

Surprise because, not only was he just 5ft 3in tall, but he had never played in an organised game of football before.

Magee was actually a rugby league player, who had found himself in the trenches of war-torn France during World War One – where he had made the acquaintance of a fellow soldier, whose best friend, it transpired, was a leading official at West Brom.

On the recommendation of that mutual friend, Magee was signed up by the club on his return from the hostilities.

Magee's debut didn't pan out too badly – he scored, and went on to make 400-odd appearances for the Albion, also winning five caps for England.

383. BOGEY MAN

Winston Bogarde, the Dutch defender signed from Barcelona by Chelsea during the 2001-02 season, was something of a misfit during his time at the club. He started four games and made eight appearances as a substitute during his first year there – and never started another game for the remainder of his four-year stay, during which time he was earning a reported £40,000 per week.

Quizzed about his value to the club, he said in 2002: 'I give my all every single day and I know that I cannot do any more than that.'

384. FOOT FETISH

During season 1938-39, when Portsmouth won the FA Cup, the team underwent a bizarre, regular ritual, in which outside right Freddie Worrall buckled a pair of white spats on to the feet of manager Jack Tinn – always left foot first – before each match.

Worrall was ultra-superstitious – he would place a tiny horseshoe in a pocket of his shorts, a sprig of heather in each sock, a coin in a boot, and pin a china elephant to a sock, for each game.

385. STRANGEST INJURY BAR NONE?

Newcastle defender Kenny Wharton suffered head and knee injuries in August 1985, having been hit by a broken crossbar.

386. FOR MY NEXT TRICK...

Patsy Gallagher scored one of the game's most unusual goals when, in the 1925 Scottish Cup final, he equalised for Celtic against Dundee by somersaulting over the line with the ball wedged between both of his feet.

387. NAKED TRUTH

Website www.royals.org invited readers to submit their own bizarre football experiences. Paul Beck contacted them to report: 'At age ten, my father took me to a game between the Hungarian national team and the Swedish national team. During the course of the game, the Swedish team scored and an elated fan jumped the fence, heading for the field, ripping off his clothes as he went.

'One of the offices stationed around the field turned his dog loose on the man. He was subdued just long enough for the officer to club his head, haul him back to the edge, and throw him back in the crowd. The officer resumed his position as if nothing had happened. To my knowledge that same fan did not see the rest of the game. For all I know he may not have ever seen a game again – he didn't seem to wake up!'

388. MAKING A SPECTACLE OF THEMSELVES

Preston keeper James Mitchell played in the 1922 FA Cup final wearing glasses – and was beaten from the penalty spot by Huddersfield's Tom Hamilton for the only goal of the game. Mitchell won an England cap in 1924.

* West Ham full-back H S Bourne, who played for the club between 1908-11, left the opposition glassy eyed – as he played wearing spectacles, as did contemporary A Raisbeck, a centre-half for Liverpool and Scotland.

* When Burslem Port Vale crashed 10-0 in a home game against Sheffield United in 1892, they blamed the result on the fact that their keeper lost his glasses in the muddy goalmouth early on in the game.

389. A COATING FOR TOMMY

Fulham director Tommy Trinder – a comic whose catchphrase was 'you lucky people' and who went to the same school, Harrow County Grammar, as your author (!), offered the generous incentive of a new overcoat to any of his side's players who hit a hat-trick during the 1947-48 season's FA Cup.

When Fulham played Bristol Rovers, their Arthur Stevens hammered three goals in the 5-2 victory, and when his third went in, Trinder hung over a balcony, waving the overcoat at him.

After the game, the FA announced an enquiry into the overcoat, investigating whether it might constitute an illegal payment, but the club got off. Maybe a cover-up was involved!

390. MILKING IT

Arsenal's George Jobey went down injured during a 1913 fixture against Leicester Fosse.

Jobey was unable to get back to his feet, and lay immobile on the pitch after treatment. The Gunners' trainer George Hardy improvised and 'had to borrow a milk cart from David Lewis, a dairyman in Gillespie Road, to wheel Jobey to his lodgings', a contemporary account recorded.

391. HANGING AROUND

American author Joe McGinnis spent a year in Italy following an obscure Serie B club for his superb book, *The Miracle of Castel di Sangro*.

McGinnis relates the shocking story of a referee hanged by fans of a team called Celano in the late 1970s.

Appalled, McGinnis asks, 'Was anyone arrested?'

'Oh no,' he is told. 'The magistrates in Rome, they all knew that the referee had been at fault.'

392. NET LOSS

Baird, the goalkeeper for Queens Park, who were taking on Rangers in the 1894 Scottish Cup semi-final, was left rooted to the spot as forward David Boyd headed the ball past him.

His hand was caught in the net.

393. HOW FOOTBALL OVERTHREW DICTATORS

The death at the age of just 27 of Romanian Second Division striker Florin Piturca, after he returned home from a December 1978 match for Drobeta Turnu Severin, affected his father Maximilian greatly.

There were rumours that the player's death occurred after he and other players were given performance-enhancing drugs to take.

Maximilian, a cobbler, built a tomb in honour of his son, erecting a specially commissioned, life-size bronze statue of him, and slept there after finishing work.

Word reached the country's dictators and in March 1989, Zoe Ceausescu of the ruling family visited the cemetery and decreed that the tomb should be removed, ordering in bulldozers.

Maximilian remained inside the tomb as it was destroyed, and emerged, screaming a curse on the Ceausescu family – 'In a year, I will be back and you will be dead!'

Within a year the Ceausescus were overthrown and executed (Zoe lived on until

2006), while the Piturca tomb was rebuilt and Maximilian resumed his nightly vigil, until his death from a heart attack in 1994.

394. OVER THE HILL?

Hill Drury, an amateur player signed by Middlesbrough towards the end of the 19th century, was so concerned about losing his amateur status that he always insisted on paying the full admission fee to get into the grounds where he played.

395. BUDGIE KILLER COLLY

Striker Stan Collymore's well-publicised problems with stress, depression and even dogging just might have had their roots in a 1996 incident which saw him being accused by a Newcastle fan of causing the death of his budgerigar.

The supporter, Dominic Hourd, wrote to Collymore – who at the time was playing for Liverpool – after he scored a late winner against Newcastle, causing Hourd and his pal Peter Phillips, watching on TV, to kick out in frustration, knocking the budgie's cage off its stand and causing the bird's sad demise.

'He can't bring Peter the budgie back,' said Hourd. 'But I told him I couldn't forgive him.'

✱ Ref Hamid Rissaoui was happy to permit East Grinstead League side The Crown to stage a minute's silence before their April 2001 game against Stone Quarry to mark a club member's bereavement. When one of the players began giggling, club skipper Phil Jarman admitted that the bereavement was that of his own pet budgie.

396. POXY COMPETITION

Middlesbrough versus Thornaby was the final of the 1898 Amateur Cup, scheduled to be played at Darlington – until residents there protested that the two Teesside-based clubs might spread to their area the smallpox epidemic that was affecting the region in which they were both based.

The FA decided on an alternative venue, but decreed that it must be kept as secret as possible, with the game being played behind closed doors to prevent objections from local residents.

So the match was played at the hill village of Brotton in Cleveland in front of a tiny turnout, with Middlesbrough running out winners of the poxy tournament.

397. CHRISTMAS LIGHTS

Some 5,000 fans dragged themselves away from their festive celebrations on Christmas night 1893, lured to Celtic's home ground to witness a unique friendly against Clyde.

For the game was to be played under floodlights – literally, as the 16 arc lights had been strung across the pitch, suspended from wires.

The experiment worked comparatively well – except when the ball was kicked into the air, when it would frequently strike the lights or the wires, causing stoppages in play.

An even earlier experiment at Kilmarnock in 1878 had resulted in player injuries when the lights failed.

In England, an experimental floodlit game took place at Sheffield United's Bramall Lane on October 14, 1878.

398. QUOIT A RECORD

Willie Cringan retired in 1925, having enjoyed a career playing for Sunderland, Celtic, Third Lanark, Motherwell and Inverness Thistle. A year later he became Scottish quoits champion.

★ Chelsea's 1921 signing, keeper Ben Howard Baker, boasted of being world high-jump record holder.

399. RUSSIAN TO CONCLUSIONS

Russian football was originally organised by exiled Brits who formed the majority of the teams there, but local objections began to grow in the early years of the 20th century; and one incident was a focal point in encouraging a growth of home-grown clubs.

In 1903 a Russian player, Chirtsov, was sent off for his team, Sport, during an incident which saw him 'almost throttled' by his opponent whilst playing against the predominantly British team, Nevsky. Chirtsov was banned for a year, while the Brit got off scot-free.

The local paper was incensed: 'The League's decision is to disqualify Chirtsov for a year and to let off Sharples with a caution! This year we had Sharples the Throttler. Next year we could have Jim the Stabber and Jack the Ripper!

'The British, in their high-handed way, having a large majority of votes, are banning a Russian who is totally innocent and letting off a man who is obviously dangerous, but one of their own. Let Russian clubs band together to form their own league. We are sure that a great future awaits football in Russia. But for that we can do with fewer Sharpleses!'

400. MIGHT HAVE ENDED IN A DRAW

Birmingham City were 16-0 ahead against Darlaston All Saints with under ten minutes remaining in an 1882 clash – when the referee abandoned the match.

401. ARRIVIDERCI GRAZI

Palermo's Graziano Ladoni was fined the equivalent of £670 in February 1971 – for refusing to say goodbye (in Italian, that is) to his manager.

402. REMIND ME, WHICH WAY ARE WE KICKING?

James Oakes and his Port Vale teammates were not best pleased when their 1932 Boxing Day fixture against Charlton was abandoned because of inclement weather.

A few weeks later the game was rescheduled and Oakes was again involved – as a Charlton player, thus becoming the first player to represent both sides in the same fixture.

403. ASKING FOR TROUBLE

The England World Cup squad released a tournament song for the 1982 competition – titled with eerie inaccuracy, *This Time (We'll Get It Right)*. Of course, they didn't (get it right).

404. REVVED UP

Kenneth Hunt and Bill Jordan, regulars at half-back and forward respectively for Wolves during the 1912-13 season, had something in common – they were both Reverend gentlemen.

405. CHILLED OUT

Wigan were 7-0 up in their Cheshire League game against Congleton on October 22, 1932 with the second half just under way, but they failed to take the points from the match, which was abandoned when five Congleton players had to leave the field suffering from exposure.

Wigan did eventually win the rearranged fixture 6-2.

406. RIGHT ROYAL SKULDUGGERY

Perhaps the earliest example of soccer skulduggery is an 1890 report that teams arriving at Shieldfield in Scotland to play local side Royal Oak, would be warned in no uncertain terms that should their goalkeeper or defenders be so misguided as to prevent the home team's star centre forward from scoring, they were liable to have the utmost difficulty in departing from the ground with their limbs intact.

407. PIZZA THE ACTION

Manchester United beat Arsenal 2-0 at Old Trafford in October 2004, and ill-feeling on the pitch spilled over into the tunnel at the end of the game, giving the football authorities food for thought as, it was reported, pizza, soup and other foodstuffs were flying about in all sorts of directions.

The Italian delicacy, reportedly aimed at United striker Ruud van Nistelrooy by an unnamed Arsenal player, missed its target and apparently came to rest on the face of Sir Alex Ferguson. Crumbs!

The furore was calmed down three days later when the two Davids – United's Gill and the Gunners' Dein, met over a 'pie and a pint', presumably kept firmly on their plates and in their glasses.

408. RUBBED UP THE WRONG WAY

Huddersfield may have rubbed up FA Cup final opponents Aston Villa the wrong way before their 1920 showdown, when they brought into their dressing room a lamp from the local pantomime production of Aladdin.

All the players rubbed the lamp for luck before they went out for the game.

Huddersfield lost 1-0. Oh yes they did!

409. NOW TELL US SOMETHING WE DON'T KNOW!

Researchers set up an experiment designed to show whether referees were biased towards home sides.

To do so they selected a game between Liverpool and Leicester at Anfield from the 1998-99 season and exposed a sample of some 40 referees to a recording of the game, half of whom watched the game with all of the crowd noise included, while the other half watched the game with the sound turned down.

The researchers concluded 'that the referees who heard the sound of the crowd were less likely to call fouls against the home team than the ones who saw the game in silence'.

They also pointed out that this 'coincided with actual decisions of the match official on the day' and concluded that 'referees tend to avoid making calls against the home team as a way of shielding themselves from the extra stress levels that come with antagonising the crowd'.

Blimey, I'd never have guessed.

★ The AA members' magazine of spring 1997 reported the unsurprising finding that research had discovered that 50 per cent would not buy a car in the colour(s) of their team's main rivals. Count me in that 50 per cent – but then who wants a yellow and red car!?

410. KZEINECAM

Notts County midfielder Neil Mackenzie became the first professional footballer to appear on Channel 4's 'Countdown' show in summer, 2008. The self-confessed crossword junkie won five consecutive contests before being defeated.

411. THAT'S THE NORM IN ALBANIA

England stars training in Tirana before their March 2001 game against Albania were surprised when a crowd of home fans arrived at the session and, ignoring the players, headed straight for 86-year-old comic Norman Wisdom.

The veteran comedian had become a huge star in Albania during the years that government censors banned all films containing violence and/or sex, but promoted all of Wisdom's corny, highly visual comic movies.

Norman didn't make the England team, which won the game 1-3.

412. I DON'T KNOW WHAT I'M DOING

With Brentford suffering an embarrassing FA Cup defeat by non-league Kingstonian, during the 2000-2001 campaign, the chairman, Ron Noades, decided that his manager was underachieving so badly that he would have to be sacked.

The manager was – himself!

413. LIGHT ENTERTAINMENT

In July 2001 the FA announced the intended introduction of a 'revolutionary' new system designed to help linesmen with offside decisions. It would consist of 'prismed lights at 1.2 metre intervals along the touchline which can only be seen when the linesman is directly opposite them'. (We're still waiting to see the light!)

414. TOO MANY FOREIGNERS?

Foreigners in British football are nothing new – Hartlepool's 1923-24 signing Tewfik Abdallah, who played 11 games for them, was an Egyptian.

415. JUST DIVINE

His nickname was 'il codino divino' – the divine ponytail – but rioting broke out in Florence when revered Italian striker Roberto Baggio was transferred to Juventus in 1990. Baggio was equally notorious for being a Buddhist.

416. WHO'LL START ME AT TWO BOB?

An auction took place at the Hotel Metropole in Leeds in 1919 – of all the PLAYERS of Leeds city, who had been expelled from the Football League for failing to permit their books to be inspected.

417. THANKS, LADS, WELL DONE

After they had qualified for the 1982 World Cup in Spain, Crown Prince Sheik Saad Abdullah Al Sabah of Kuwait gave each of his nation's 24 players a Cadillac, a villa, a plot of land, a gold watch, and a speedboat. No cuddly toys then?

418. WHOSE BENEFIT IS THAT?

FRANK STOKES well deserved the benefit match he was awarded by his club, Birmingham, after playing 199 games for them in the seven seasons leading up to 1910.

The right-back anticipated receiving the acclaim of the crowd – and a decent cash handout, too – at the game.

However, Stokes was dumbfounded to discover that he had been selected for Birmingham reserves in a match taking place on the same day as his benefit, which he was consequently unable to take part in.

419. BARCA LONER

Swiss footballer Joan Gamper, 21, captain of FC Basel was, in 1898, on his way to Africa, so stopped off in Barcelona to visit an uncle.

He loved the city and decided to stay, placing an advertisement in a local paper on October 22, 1899 inviting like-minded people to help him form a football club.

The red and blue strip he selected for the new FC Barcelona was similar to the FC Basel outfit – the club badges are also remarkably similar.

Gamper became founder, player, skipper and president, but in 1925 fans in the Catalan city jeered the Spanish national anthem at Barca games – and Gamper was accused of stirring up Catalan nationalism and expelled from the country.

Back home in Switzerland, depressed and strapped for cash, he committed suicide in 1930, aged 53.

★ In 2007 it was reported that Barcelona replica shorts being sold in Saudi Arabia had to bear a different club badge. In order to make them 'religiously correct', the red cross on white background was changed to a vertical red stripe.

420. YOU'VE GOAT TO LAUGH

Watford were attacking during a 1909 fixture at their then Cassio Road ground when, explained a match report, a goat encroached on to the pitch and, 'in certain of its actions, spoke eloquently of its disgust for the whole dull and uneventful proceedings'.

Some things never change.

421. BEASTLIE FURIE

'Footeballe, wherein is nothinge but beastlie furie and extreme violence, whereof procedeth hurte and consequently rancour, and malice do remaine with them that be wounded'. As accurate today as it was when he wrote it – Thomas Elyot, 1531.

422. BOOTED BARBARIANS

'London witnessed an incursion of Northern barbarians – hot-blooded Lancastrians, sharp of tongue, rough and ready, of uncouth garb and speech. A tribe of Soudanese [sic] Arabs let loose in the stand would not excite more amusement and curiosity.' Parochial observations by the London-based *Pall Mall Gazette* as Blackburn Rovers fans visited the capital to see the 1884 Cup final.

423. SOFTY

'We have discovered since the match that the air at Ascot was not bracing enough. It was what might be termed 'softening'. It tended to reduce the stamina of the men.' A novel excuse by WBA secretary Mr Smith to explain how his team, who had prepared for the 1887 FA Cup final against Aston Villa by staying at an Ascot hotel, had managed to lose.

424. IF ONLY THEY'D LISTENED

'The practice of buying and selling players is unsportsmanlike and most objectionable'. Sir Charles Clegg of the FA in 1899.

425. GENERAL TURNCOAT

'I started cheering for the Blues, but when I saw the Reds winning I had to go on cheering for the Reds.' Every football supporter has met 'fans' like General Eisenhower, who took time off from winning the war to visit the 1944 Cup final in which Charlton, the Reds, beat the Blues, Chelsea, 3-1.

426. BY GUM

'Chewing gum. Always use it. Put some on my hands. Rub it well in.' Jack Kelsey, Welsh international keeper of the 1950s.

427. ARMLESS ENOUGH

Hector Castro, goalscorer for Uruguay in the 1930 World Cup final, had lost the lower part of one arm.

In December 2005 Paraguay and Vicenza striker Julio Gonzalez had his left arm amputated after a car accident. In December 2007 he returned to the professional game, playing for Tacuary in their 1-1 draw at Olimpia in the Paraguayan League. He did not wear his prosthetic arm.

428. BALD TRUTH

Rangers manager Dick Advocaat revealed in March 2000 that he had gone into the transfer market with a hair-raising scheme – the transfer of thousands of hairs from the back of to the top of his head.

The 52-year-old Dutchman had permitted 'before' and 'after' shots of his tonsure to be used in advertisements for Dutch hair company Laser Aesthetic, and said: 'I have nothing against people who are bald, but I feel better with hair than without.'

★ Bulgarian international keeper Boris Mikhailov joined Reading in the 1990s and gave opposing fans much entertainment by achieving many hair-raising saves while performing under his rather obvious hair-piece or toupee.

429. BOARD STIFF

Milan Rapaic of Hadjuk Split was ruled out of action during the 1999-2000 season after sticking a plane boarding pass in his eye.

430. WILL POWER

Brazilian club Bangu received a totally unexpected cash windfall in 1984 when a mathematics professor with no readily apparent connection to them left them £250,000 in his will.

Mystified, the club learned that the man – who insisted that he should remain anonymous – had once attended a carnival in the town, where he had met and fallen in love with a beautiful young girl.

Having no close relatives to whom he could leave his wealth, he opted for the club connected with the love of his life.

* Yorky Whiting, a Fulham fan who died in 1966, left the club a house painted in Fulham's colours – and in 1998 60-year-old Ken Selwyn willed cash-strapped Gloucester City his £73,000 house.

431. THE FIRST ...

* ref to send himself off may have been Melvin Sylvester who, in 1998, 'lost it completely' and punched a player while officiating at a Hampshire League game, and then red-carded himself.

* ref stretchered off at Wembley Stadium was Alan Wilkie, who collapsed with a calf injury during the second half of the 1999-2000 Worthington Cup final between Leicester and Tranmere.

* female linesman at Wembley Stadium – Wendy Toms in the 1999-2000 Worthington Cup final.

* outfield player to reach 1,000 senior appearances – Tony Ford, 41, who achieved it turning out for Rochdale in an Auto Windscreens Shield match on March 7, 2000.

* goalscorer direct from a corner was Huddersfield's Billy Smith in October 1924.

* team to score 3,000 First Division goals was Everton when on October 7, 1980 they beat Brighton 3-1.

* player 'done' for feigning injury was Gordon Durie of Spurs, who received

a three-match ban for the offence in October 1992 – although it was later rescinded on appeal. So the FA was feigning his guilt, then!

* player to score an own goal – George Cox of Aston Villa versus Wolves on November 8, 1888.

* 18-year-old playing for England to be knocked unconscious, Michael Owen in 1998 versus Morocco.

* club to win Premier League whose first colours were anything other than red – Blackburn Rovers in 1995.

* club to 'sell its soul' by allowing big business to buy the name of its stadium – Scarborough FC in 1988 changed their ground's name to the McCain Stadium, chipping away at tradition in the process.

* son to come on as sub for his dad in an international – Eidur Gudjohnsen, who replaced Arnor for Iceland during their 3-0 1996 win over Estonia.

432. GLASSY-EYED

Ayr United fan Jason Stuart, 28, was fined £100 in February 2000 after he had become agitated when his side conceded a goal against Celtic the previous December – and threw his glasses on to the pitch.

* Belgian star Joseph 'Jef' Jurion won 64 caps in the 1960s despite having to play wearing specially designed spectacles with unbreakable lenses, soft frames and rubber straps.

433. HAIR TODAY ...

'After I had my hair cut someone went through the bins of Toni and Guy in London. Maybe they were going to sell it.' David Beckham's April 2000 quote revealed the absurd lengths to which fan s were prepared to go to get close to – or to scalp in the memorabilia market, perhaps – their idol.

434. I'LL BE DOGGONE – OR NOT

Jan van Kook, 33, bought a season ticket to watch matches at Feyenoord in season 1999-2000 – for his dog, Bo.

435. LIGHT RELIEF

Stephane Porato, Marseille keeper, fell off a chair and injured ligaments during the 1999-2000 season – while he was trying to change a lightbulb.

436. PILES OF PROBLEMS

Brazilian player Ramalho was confined to bed for three days during the 1999-2000 season after swallowing a suppository.

437. PISSED OFF

A vital local cup tie in April 2000 between Norwegian sides Surnadal and Sunndale was won by a shot from halfway by Sunndale's striker – who spotted Surnadal keeper Olav Fiske temporarily indisposed while taking a pee on the touchline.

Attempting to relieve himself of blame, Fiske merely succeeded in wetting himself as he dashed for the ball. He commented: 'This situation caused me a great deal of embarrassment.'

438. ROVERS AND OUT

Teenager David Stephenson Ingham Brennan Newton Noble Waldron Thompson Flynn Rodaway Hankin Collins James Welch plucked up the courage to tell his Burnley-loving family, including mother, Gillian, who named him after their 1974–75 team, that he was actually a Blackburn fan. 'They took it really badly,' he said, plaintively, in April 2000.

439. TAYLOR MAID

Airdrie fan Eric Boslem of Lanarkshire named his new daughter Taylor Airdrie Elizabeth in February 2000 – despite her mum, Margaret, being a Rangers fan.

440. WRESTLEMANIA

Manchester United striker Ole Gunnar Solskjaer's father Oivind was Norway's Greco-Roman wrestling champion from 1966-71.

∗ Former Ipswich striker Kevin Beattie defeated Sylvester Stallone in an arm-wrestling competition during filming for movie *Escape to Victory*. 'He was an arrogant sod,' said Beattie.

441. ON YER BIKE, MATE – OH, DEAR ...

Pedro Gatica from Argentina set off to cycle his way to Mexico to see his country play in the 1986 World Cup.

When the 52-year-old finally, sore of rear, got there he discovered that he did not have enough money left to get into Argentina's next match.

And while he tried to persuade someone to give him a ticket, thieves stole his bike.

442. GOODCHILD – NOT SUCH
A GOOD DANCER

Half-time entertainment was perhaps somewhat more exotic back in the 1920s than today – and Watford's star turn in those days was tap dancer Joey Goodchild, who would tap away on the roof of the main stand so that everyone could get a good view.

Health and safety would have kittens today – and with good reason, as Goodchild's terpsichorean efforts came to a sudden end when, during one game, he teetered on the guttering at the edge of the rood, before toppling over, plummeting down, bouncing off an unfortunate gentleman spectator, breaking his glasses in the process, before landing on a nearby female fan, who could have done without the excitement.

Watford smoothed over the incident by apologising to the gent and paying the woman £25 in compensation.

443. LINESWOMAN'S NEW STRIP

Brazilian linesman, er, lineswoman, er, linesperson, Paula Oliveira became a controversial figure when she wrongly ruled out a goal during a Copa Brasil match in May 2007, resulting in a three- game suspension.

Feeling that she had been frozen out of major games ever since, she found a novel way to register her annoyance – by stripping off for a *Playboy* magazine photo-shoot for its July 2007 edition.

The 29-year-old women's rights campaigner was reportedly paid £125,000 for the pictures, so probably was not over-concerned when referees' boss Edson Rezende suggested that it could be bad for her future football career and when fellow female lineswoman Aline Lambert commented that posing naked might be seen as 'incompatible with the profession'.

444. WIGAN GOT THE BLUES

Traditionally playing in red and white, Wigan fell on hard times when they finished bottom of the Cheshire League in the 1945-46 season. With the restrictions of wartime still biting, the club was forced to adopt new colours when the sports shop supplying the club was unable to locate a red and white strip, forcing them to switch to blue, which was all they could supply.

445. FOOTBALL'S MOST DAMAGING QUOTE

Ashley Cole must have thought it would engage people's sympathies if he included in his autobiography an explanation of how he felt to be undervalued by Arsenal.

Explaining how he had learned that his employers had decided to refuse to accede to his request for a wage packet of £60,000 per week, Cole revealed how he had reacted when his agent gave him the news while he was at the wheel of his Bentley Continental motor car.

'I nearly swerved off the road,' he declared in his ghostwritten autobiography, *My Defence*. '"He is taking the piss, Jonathan"' I yelled down the phone. I was so incensed. I was trembling with anger. I couldn't believe what I'd heard.'

Of course, he couldn't – wouldn't we all have reacted in the same way when discovering that we would not be offered any more than a paltry £55,000 per week?

Well, no, most of us wouldn't and Ashley was soon held up to ridicule as a result.

However, he almost shook off the stigma when in early 2008 he was accused of being unfaithful to his partner Cheryl and was instead linked with a story that while, er, comforting another female companion, he had vomited on her cream carpet. However, being a true gentleman, he allegedly was gallant enough to wash his mouth out before continuing to comfort his companion, who later complained: 'He slapped my backside so hard his wedding ring left an imprint.' How she could see this imprint was not explained.

446. HEGAN HE-MAN

Ace forward Lieutenant K E Hegan was a star player for Corinthians in their 1930 FA Cup struggles against Millwall, when the amateurs fought out a 2-2 draw before meeting four days later at Second Division Millwall's New Cross ground for the replay.

'The Army officer found himself as direct a target as the ball. He may have been excused for believing himself in a commando raid instead of a cup tie,' reported his contemporary, Edward Grayson, 'for he was so roughly treated and knocked about, that he found out afterwards that he had played throughout the last 85 minutes with a broken tibia!'

Eat your heart out, Bert Trautmann – almost an entire game with a broken leg and even then he laid on the opening goal for teammate R W V Robins as the amateurs were then pegged back, but again made the running and almost stole the game in extra-time.

The second replay took place without Hegan – who was laid up in hospital as his teammates were level at 1-1 at half-time but eventually crashed out 5-1, causing *The Times* to observe, after a combined crowd of 140,000 had watched the three games, that: 'Not a little of the play of Millwall was of a nature not likely to attract fresh followers.'

447. BEATLING ABOUT

Beatle fans in the crowd were amused in November 2007 as Spurs, with Lennon in their side, lined up against West Ham, with McCartney in theirs.

448. CIG-NATURE?

An art lover paid £5,280 for an empty packet of Woodbines cigarettes in November 2007. On it in pencil was sketched a doodle featuring figures playing football in an industrial landscape.

The sketching was done by artist L S Lowry.

449. NOT EVEN A NEW STRIP?

Spanish women's side Torrejon were so desperate to attract a sponsorship deal that the side stripped off for a full-frontal photo shoot which appeared in the *El Pais* publication in October 2007.

However, they still failed to attract a deal, leaving a club official commenting: 'We went nude for all the right reasons.'

450. TAGETHER

On parole after being jailed for drink-driving in 2005, Birmingham City's Jermaine Pennant made his debut wearing an electronic tag.

451. ENLISTING OUTSIDE HELP

With England set to play Sweden in the 2002 World Cup with a 10am kick-off English-time, devout fans were concerned about having to choose between God and country – until the Archbishop of Canterbury, George Carey, himself an Arsenal fan, stepped in to announce special dispensation for altered Sunday morning church service times.

God clearly had mixed feelings about this move – England could only draw 1-1.

452. MIKE LINED UP FOR JOB

In one of the most bizarre selection methods ever employed to choose a new manager, Luton Town fans were offered the opportunity of telephoning the club with their choice of boss in June 2003.

The phone vote was operated by controversial new club chairman John Gurney, who was also talking about amalgamating the club with Wimbledon and incorporating a new Grand Prix circuit in plans for a new ground.

He announced the result of his telephone poll on June 23, shortly after the lines had closed and, oddly enough, the winner Mike Newell was wheeled out and introduced to the media, despite fan websites and fanzines insisting that their own soundings suggested that the current manager Joe Kinnear should have come out on top.

453. ONE-EYED REACTION
TO NELSON

With England in South Africa for a May 2003 international, a dozen players were delighted to attend a meeting in Johannesburg with Nelson Mandela.

Eight, though, were not – and remained in their hotel, reportedly 'catching up on some sleep'.

454. HULLO, HULLO?

Hull City's 2002 sponsors Kingston Communications handed out mobiles to staff and players as part of the deal.

Sadly, due to a lack of network coverage in and around the ground area they weren't a great deal of use.

455. WE WERE BRILLIANT, BUT...

'We had 500 passes, they had 222. We had 18 shots on goal, they had 12. We had 64 per cent of possession. That sums up the game.'

Arsene Wenger was in no doubt about which was the better side in the 2008 Carling Cup semi-final second leg game against Spurs which they, er, won, perhaps? No.

They lost 5-1.

456. DRAX THE WAY TO DO IT – PERHAPS.

Baffled by his side Maidenhead United's continuing terrible home form – just one win in front of their own fans all season, compared with five on the road – manager Johnson 'Drax' Hippolyte came up with a plan to put matters straight.

He treated the late January 2008 home game against Braintree as though it were an away match and made players meet up well before kick-off time, before loading them aboard their away game coach for a trip around the town, arriving back at the ground in time to prepare for the game.

Drax had used the technique before, successfully, when he was with renowned FA Cup giant-killers Yeading. 'I hoped it would relax the players before the game,' he said.

It may have relaxed them too much. They lost 1-0.

457. DEAD RIGHT, THERE

Speaking about Spurs boss Martin Jol, who had just been sacked, BBC pundit and former player Steve Claridge commented: 'Martin Jol was literally a dead man walking at Spurs.'

458. HUNT THE DRAGON

Andy Hunt was a successful striker for Charlton Athletic and had previously been so for Newcastle when, it seemed almost overnight, he disappeared from the game at the end of the 1999-2000 season.

He had fallen victim to Chronic Fatigue Syndrome and, boy, did he ever disappear.

To the jungle of Belize, in fact – which is where he is to this day, running Green Adventure Travel and the Belize Jungle Dome, together with his partner Simone Engeln, a Dutch former MTV 'Veejay' with whom he has two children.

Andy had become aware of his problem in September 2000 after a game against Spurs, when 'I was supposed to go to a friend's wedding reception, but physically I couldn't move'.

Two games later, against Coventry, a shot hit the bar and bounced towards Hunt, 15 yards out – 'I just flopped forwards to head it and scored. That was it, they substituted me and I never played again.'

Hunt discovered Belize when he went online looking for a retreat. He went over there and bought himself a seven-bedroomed wooden dome alongside a riverbank in the jungle and began to plan a business selling books, coffee, smoothies and health food, grown on their own 1,000-acre farm.

You will find details of his current businesses at www.greendragonbelize.com. Here is a sample of what the site says about Andy and Simone:

'Between them they have travelled much of the world and they have a passion and unique knowledge of what the adventure traveller desires without sacrificing the comfort required for an enjoyable vacation. They have developed an unrivalled resort atmosphere at the Belize Jungle Dome and invite you to experience the beauty and diversity of Belize. Often called Mother Nature's Best Kept Secret.'

Andy quit the game at the age of 30, but still keeps in touch with it and writes a regular blog about issues within football, reachable via the Green Dragon site.

459. WEREN'T YOU ONCE
A FOOTBALLER?

* Eamonn Bannon, former Scotland midfielder, took over the Strathallan Guest House in Edinburgh in 1997.

* Gudni Bergsson, once of Spurs and Bolton, became a lawyer in his native Iceland.

* Clyde Best of West Ham joined the Bermuda Prison Service in 1999.

* Alan Comfort, former Cambridge United, Orient and Middlesbrough winger, became a vicar.

* Gordon Davies, former Fulham player, opened a pest control business.

* Jim Doherty, former Motherwell and Notts County forward, was a deep sea diver, checking steel cables on oil rigs worldwide in 2008.

* Marco Gabbiadini, formerly of Sunderland, Derby and Crystal Palace was, in 2007, running Bishops, a guest house, in York.

* Micky Gynn, part of Coventry's 1987 FA Cup winning team was, in early 2008, a postman, in common with other former star players Neil Webb, Kevin Hector and former Scottish Cup winner Derek McKay. Gynn is also a soul music DJ.

* Micky Hazard, once of Spurs and Chelsea, became a London black cab driver.

* Klas Ingesson, from Sweden, played for Sheffield Wednesday before retiring from the game to become a lumberjack.

* Brian Kilcline, who captained Coventry to win the 1987 FA Cup final, was reported in January 2008 to be a professional arm-wrestler.

* Don Masson, former Scotland, Notts County and QPR midfielder, was running The Grange guesthouse near Newark in 2008.

* David May, former Blackburn and Manchester United defender, launched his own wine label, Mayson Ridge, when he began importing and selling wine from South Africa.

* Adrian Sprott, of Hamilton Academicals in the 1980s, is now in charge of lost property for Lothian and Borders police.

* Ray Stewart of Dundee United, West Ham, St Johnstone and Stirling Albion, retired in 2004, becoming a chauffeur.

* Alan Taylor of West Ham, Norwich and Cambridge United has been both milkman and newsagent since retiring in 1989.

* Michael Thomas of Arsenal and Liverpool went into 'security' – 'We guard presidents and things like that.'

* Ian Ure, Scottish international, retired in the 1970s and became a social worker.

* Pak Doo Ik, goalscoring hero of North Korea's 1966 World Cup finals victory over Italy, gave up football to become a dentist.

* Andy Ansah of Southend is now a 'football consultant' for Hollywood and Bollywood films such as the *Goal!* trilogy and '*Dhana Dhan Goal*'.

460. SCOUTS NOT PREPARED FOR FOOTBALL

'Football is a vicious game when it draws mere onlookers at few paid performers, thousands of boys and young men, pale, narrow chested, hunched up, miserable specimens, smoking endless cigarettes, betting, learning to be hysterical as they groan or cheer in panic unison with their neighbours.'

It would seem fair to suggest that the founder of the Boy Scout movement, Lord Baden-Powell, was not a great football fan, judging by this outburst in the 1908 book, *Scouting For Boys*.

461. SWIFT HALF?

Wales were playing in the town of Baku in the former Soviet republic of Azerbaijan in November 2002. Accompanying the team, a *Daily Telegraph* reporter described their destination as 'one of the most remote and inhospitable imaginable'.

But he felt more at home when he discovered that, close to the ground, was an English-style pub named the Lancaster Gate, boasting a sign featuring the FA's three lions' crest, and featuring an interior packed with British football memorabilia.

462. LICKING THE OPPOSITION

Plymouth Argyle claimed to be the first club to produce ice-cream in club colours when, in February 2008, they handed out thousands of tubs of green and white ice cream, called Pilgrims' Passion, during their home game against Hull.

But, although the ice-cream may have scooped up plaudits, they were frozen out and licked on the pitch, going down to a 0-1 defeat.

463. GRAVE CONCERNS

Inter Milan supporter Massimo Pecorino, 52, was so distraught every time his team lost an important game that he began to erect a gravestone on his local mountainside to mark each defeat.

By July 2007 there were more than 20 gravestones at the site in Cortona.

Pecorino said that he had begun the bizarre ritual after a particularly hard-to-take defeat. 'Instead of enjoying a celebration, I felt like I was at a funeral, so I spent the day carving out my fury on a stone.'.

Had I emulated his actions during my own team Luton Town's ill-fated 2007-08 League One campaign I would have created a whole packed cemetery at my local landmark, Harrow on the Hill!

464. CASUAL DECISION?

In 2000, the World Intellectual Property Organisation (WIPO) ordered Sallen Enterprises, the operators of a website devoted to St Paul's correspondence with the residents of Corinth, to hand over the domain name corinthians.com to the Brazilian soccer club, Corinthians.

The fact that the Pauline epistles predated the Sao Paulo team (founded in 1910) by some 1,865 years apparently cut little ice with the WIPO. A one-man panel found that 'the posting was fabricated to divert consumers, or more generally the public interested in visiting what they think is the site of the well-known Brazilian soccer team'.

The decision went down like a lead balloon in Christian circles but no plague or famine has yet been visited on the football team as a result.

465. AIMING HIGH

Argonauts FC, an amateur side formed in 1928 from the ashes of a club that had contested – unsuccessfully, as they crashed out in round one – the 1879-80 FA Cup, had high ambitions.

Having failed to be accepted for immediate membership of the Football League as they had no track record behind them at all, they decided to try to impress the powers-that-be with their home ground – so, in 1930, they made a provisional booking of Wembley Stadium to host their home matches.

When the time came for the votes to be counted to discover whether they would get in to the Third Division South, they were distraught to discover that they had polled a total of no votes whatsoever.

466. GOOD NUDES FOR BRAZIL

Rosemary de Mello, a 24-year-old secretary, wound up posing nude in the Brazilian edition of *Playboy* after she threw a firework on to the pitch during a vital World Cup qualifier between her team Brazil and Chile, played in September 1989.

The firework landed alongside Chilean keeper Roberto Rojas, who crumpled to the ground and was carried off the field by teammates with red staining his face. Brazil were a goal up and there were 21 minutes left.

The Chilean team refused to carry on and left the field.

However, Brazil were eventually awarded a 2-0 forfeit victory as Rojas's injuries turned out to be fake. The Chilean trainer and several top football officials resigned or were fired. Rojas was banned for life by FIFA, and Chile from the 1994 World Cup. Brazil were, however, fined $31,000 because of the fireworks.

Their national federation tried to make de Mello pay the fine.

467. NOT SO SACROSANCT NOW

An offer of £2 million in January 1992 for sponsorship of the FA Cup competition by Bass Breweries was turned down flat.

FA chairman Bert Millichip huffed that the Cup was 'sacrosanct'.

On February 19, 1992, Bass Breweries agreed a reported £12 million sponsorship of the FA Premier League, to be known as the Carling Premiership.

468. THAT'S LOYALTY

Wrexham reserves attracted a record crowd of 18,069 for their match against Wisford United in January 1957.

What? Oh, yes, there was a reason – tickets for a forthcoming cup tie went on sale that night. They were playing Manchester United.

469. SIXTY-FOUR CAPS – BUT HE WASN'T QUALIFIED TO PLAY

Tony Cascarino played 64 times for the Republic of Ireland – and then discovered he wasn't qualified to play for them, yet still won a further 24 caps.

In his autobiography, *Full Time,* published in 2000 and shortlisted for the prestigious William Hill Sports Book of the Year, Cascarino said that he could have played for Italy, England and Scotland, but opted for the Republic in 1985. 'I suppose because they chose me – I qualified under the 'grandparents' rule. My mother, Theresa O'Malley, was the youngest of four daughters born to Agnes and Michael Joseph O'Malley, a native of Westport, County Mayo.'

Cascarino duly used this qualification to achieve selection for the country, despite being unable to acquire an Irish passport for what he assumed were technical reasons.

In 1996 the rules for qualification changed. An Irish passport was now essential.

And his mother admitted to him that she was not the child of Michael O'Malley.

Cascarino 'decided to brave it out' and applied for the passport – which was granted. 'I was an official Irishman.'

470. MIGHT HAVE GUESSED

Chelsea must have known they were asking for trouble when they gave Scottish keeper Les Fridge his debut at home to Watford on May 5, 1986 – and sure enough, he froze and conceded five goals.

It was cold comfort that no-one held him responsible – well, they did, actually. He was frozen out after that and never played for the first team again.

471. IT'LL COST YOU

Cardiff manager Alan Durban turned down the request from Reading striker Trevor Senior after their match on September 2, 1985, to keep the match ball after he had hit a hat-trick past the Welshmen.

'If he wants to give us £40 then he can have it,' said Durban.

472. JUST ANOTHER RUN-OF-THE-MILL SEASON

Colombian football has endured many problems unknown in other countries, most notoriously the fatal shooting of full-back Andres Escobar on his return from the 1994 World Cup. In 1989 the season was cancelled after referee Alvaro Ortega was shot, reportedly on cartel orders, after the arbiter had allegedly failed to ensure a result they wanted. The 2001 season was a vintage example as:

★ Millonarios players received death threats.

★ Atletico Nacional had to train in secret after angry fans attacked players at their usual training ground.

★ Caldas players were injured when a bomb went off in Cali before a match with the US.

★ Internationals Norberto Cadavid, formerly of the US, and ex-Deportivo Cali star Aldemar Sanchez were both shot dead.

473. ULTIMATE TRIBUTE

It seems unlikely that Steve McClaren will get one, but when Ukraine's greatest ever international coach Valeri Lobanovsky, who had coached Dynamo Kiev and both the Russian and Ukrainian national teams over a 40-year period, died in May 2002, his passing was marked by a state funeral.

His body had also lain in state in Dynamo's stadium where 100,000 paid their last respects.

474. LOWERED THE TONE

Manchester City, then in the First Division, were awarded a penalty during their home 1967-68 FA Cup tie against Third Division side Reading. Penalty specialist Francis Lee placed the ball on the spot and turned to take his usual lengthy run-up to hit the ball.

As he started on his walk back, left-wing teammate Tony Coleman decided that he wanted to take the spot kick and duly ran up and belted the ball goalwards before Lee had even turned to start his run-up.

Coleman's kick sailed over the bar and the game ended 0-0, but Coleman had the last laugh, scoring in the 7-0 replay win while Lee failed to get on the scoresheet.

475. SEW WHAT? WORLD CUP STRANGENESS

During the 2006 World Cup, two lifers in a Bulgarian jail demanded a TV to watch matches on.

When their request was refused they went on hunger strike, sewing their mouths up.

Whether they ever got their telly is unrecorded.

Meanwhile, at the tournament in Germany, Dutch supporters were forced to watch their country's game against Ivory Coast in their underpants, after their traditional orange lederhosen, emblazoned with the name of a Dutch beer, were confiscated by stadium officials in Stuttgart on the grounds that the brewery was not an official tournament sponsor.

A reported 1,000 or more fans were de-trousered, and the offending garments were thrown into rubbish bins.

* Czech Republic players demanded that their hotel hire a Czech chef to prepare Knedilky dumplings for them.

* Cambodian monks permitted to watch World Cup games on television were warned by their superiors that they would be thrown out of the order should they 'cheer or make noise'.

* Ukraine coach Oleg Blokhin endeavoured to encourage his players' efforts by promising to lift their sex ban if they reached the semi-finals. They didn't. However, Italy boss Marcello Lippi took the opposite approach – not only did he impose a sex ban, he had porn channels removed from his players' hotel televisions. They won the tournament.

* Bangladeshi politicians demanded that parliamentary sessions should be cut short during the World Cup.

* Togo coach Otto Pfister, 68, resigned, returned, walked out again and then turned up for their opening match wearing jeans and a medallion, flouting the FIFA no-smoking policy by puffing away during Togo's game against Switzerland. Meanwhile, his team fought over money, threatening not to play if they didn't get the cash they wanted and then celebrated the only goal they scored by doing bunny hops.

* World Cup mascot Goleo the Lion was a complete flop – the company that held the rights to produce replicas reportedly went bust, while the 8ft lion's trouserless appearances led to complaints by German mothers' groups that he was indecent.

★ Croatia reacted to defeat by Brazil in their opening game by going to see heavy rockers Deep Purple play – 'music gets the rhythm process going and the bloodstream flowing,' claimed a Croatian FA spokesman.

476. HEADS YOU WIN

Defender Graham Capstick, 19, claimed a world record after heading a goal from an estimated 57 yards out.

Playing for Holker Old Boys in Barrow-in-Furness, Cumbria, in April 2007, the 6ft 3in Manchester United fan had leaped to head a clearance from the opposing keeper back in his direction – only for the ball to soar back towards the goal and bounce over the keeper into the net.

The goal was submitted to Guinness World Records to see whether it was an all-time best. However, in September 1998, 22-year-old Allistair Lang headed home from an estimated 60 yards while playing for Northbank against Spital Rovers in the Northern Alliance League.

At that time the FA said that the longest scoring header they were aware of was from Peter Aldis for Aston Villa against Sunderland in 1952, from a mere 35 yards out.

477. SOLID GOLD SPORTSMAN

Norwich centre-forward Percy Varco believed in playing the game 'the right way' so when, during the 1920s, he 'scored' a goal he knew should have been ruled out, he told the referee, who duly disallowed it.

Instead of being torn from limb to limb, he was feted and congratulated, with club chairman Ernie Morse presenting him with a gold sovereign for his act of outstanding sportsmanship.

Varco, 1905-82, went on to play for QPR and Exeter.

478. TICKET TO HEAVEN

Cardinal Thomas Winning, a popular Scottish religious figure who died in 2001, was laid to rest with his ticket from a Celtic cup final victory up his sleeve – placed there by his nephew before the June funeral.

479. GIVE HIM AN OSCAR!

Sarcastic fans often call for diving players to be given an Oscar for their play-acting abilities.

Dundee United's 1936-37 skipper Neal Paterson did actually win an Oscar, albeit in 1960, after he had quit the game. But he had become a Hollywood screenplay writer – and bagged his statue for his work on the movie *Room At The Top*. That title proved apt for his old side who, a few weeks later, were promoted to Division One.

480. WHAT A BOHR

Nils Bohr was a member of the Danish Olympic football squad that won silver medals at both the 1908 and 1912 Games.

He did rather well after giving up the game –becoming a professor at Copenhagen University, and the only Dane ever to win the Nobel Prize for physics.

Bohr may have set the standards for the Norwegian game – their national team manager from 1990-98, Egil Olsen, was a professor of economics.

✱ Perhaps the most notable British equivalent is the player known as E.F.Buzzard when he scored in the first ever FA Amateur Cup final in 1895 (one of three in which he played) for Old Carthusians, who beat Casuals 2-1 – a game in which, incidentally, Casuals left-back L V Lodge was ten minutes late in joining due to the late running of his train from Cambridge. Buzzard, then much more grandly known as Sir E Farquhar Buzzard, Regius Professor of Medicine at Cambridge University, was later appointed Physician to King George VI.

481. HAMMERED FOR A DRINK

Four high-profile West Ham players went out for a drink in a nightclub – no 'roasting', no fighting, no drugs – before an FA Cup tie against Blackpool, on New Year's Day, 1970, which they then lost.

The players – England skipper Bobby Moore; Jimmy Greaves, Brian Dear and Clyde Best – were all fined and dropped by the Hammers.

However, the news of the players' suspension was withheld – in order not to spoil Bobby Moore's appearance on TV's top-rated show, *This Is Your Life*, in which presenter Eamonn Andrews eulogised the legendary player, and handed over the traditional big red book to mark the occasion.

Worse was to come, when Moore was then dropped from the England squad for the first time since Sir Alf Ramsey became manager in 1962.

Greaves, who said that the players had visited boxer Brian London's nightclub 'for a couple of hours', where they 'drank a few lagers' was outraged by his and the other players' treatment: 'I was appalled by the treatment Bobby Moore got. What the critics and commentators did to him was as sickening a case of kicking a man while he is down that I can recall. It's probably the only incident in my career that I felt deeply bitter about.'

Greaves was also critical of Ramsey who, he felt, 'dropped Bobby just when Bobby needed his support most of all'.

482. BILL'S UNIQUE HAT-TRICK

Stockport skipper Bill Bocking played the last of 276 games for County in April 1931 in a Third Division North game against Wrexham. He was transferred to Second Division Everton and made his debut against Preston in their last game of the season, in which they were crowned champions.

His next game was their first in the First Division against Birmingham City – so he had played in all three divisions in consecutive games.

483. TIBET OR NOT TO BET

Tibet's exiled football team won their first match in eight years in late 2007, beating the Imphal West District FA in the All India Governor's Gold Cup. They wore tasteful white, sponsored shirts bearing the legend 'Tibet – you bet – mybet.de', promoting a German internet bookie.

484. PUT IN THE PICTURES

Jack Connor and his wife settled down to watch the film in the Bradford cinema where they had gone to spend the evening on October 19, 1951.

Suddenly a message was flashed up on the screen – 'Would Jack Connor, Bradford City's centre forward, please go to the foyer.'

Wondering whether he was going to be handed a free ice-cream or thrown out for being under age, Jack duly made his way out and was met by Stockport County manager Andy Beattie and the club's chairman, Ernest Barlow – who talked Jack into signing for them there and then for a fee of £2,500.

* Sheffield United forward Ernest Marshall was so coveted by Cardiff City manager Cyril Spiers that when the player's contract lapsed he turned up at his house at midnight on May 7, 1939, got Ernest out of bed in his pyjamas, and insisted on getting his signature.

* Brian Clough spent the night sleeping in the spare room at Preston player Archie Gemmill's home on September 22, 1970 – so that he could land his £60,000 transfer target for Derby first thing in the morning before any other club could try to buy him.

485. WHAT A WAY FOR BULLY TO GO

Napoleon the Bull, Hereford United's mascot – a real one, not a fan in fancy dress – met a tragic but probably pleasurable end at the age of four in February 2000 while performing mating duties with a heifer.

The huge beast, paraded regularly before the crowd prior to cup matches, suffered a fatal injury and was put down.

A suggestion that the bull should be commemorated by being consumed at a celebration dinner was dismissed by shocked club officials who declared the idea to be 'in the worst possible taste'.

* Sir Alex Ferguson's appointment as a Freeman of the City of Manchester gives him the right to drive cattle through the city centre.

486. KING CYNIC OF THE COUNTRY
OF CYNICAMERICA

Cynicism and football seem to have gone hand in hand for some while, yet it is still possible even now to be astonished at the depths of cynicism to which some football figures will resort.

Step forward this volume's own King Cynic of Cynicamerica, the most cynical of football cynics – will you welcome Eurico Miranda, president of Brazil's Vasco club.

Vasco were playing Sao Caetano in their 2000 championship play-off. More fans than was healthy for their own safety and that of the Sao Januario stadium packed in to see the game.

Overcrowding and other chaotic situations led to a huge terrace crush, causing every sensible and responsible person present to call for the abandonment of the game.

But, even as hundreds of injured people were crying for help, Miranda was trying to order ambulances and helicopters away, insisting that all was well and the match should be concluded.

This attitude might just have been related to the fact that Vasco were leading at the time.

Common sense and decency eventually prevailed and the game was halted and abandoned, and the emergency services permitted to get on with their life-saving work – at which point Vasco changed tack and claimed the trophy.

487. TAKE A DEEP BREATH

Half-time refreshments at Peruvian club Union Minas are unique, in that along with oranges, tea and all the usual stuff, they also provide oxygen for players. The club play in the Andes, near Bolivia, at 4,380m – the highest altitude in the world – so breathless thrills are commonplace in games here!

∗ In May 2007 FIFA imposed a ban on International games being played above 2,500m, but were forced to raise the limit to 3,000m after complaints from the South American Federation, and then introduced a dispensation to permit Bolivia to play at La Paz, which is at 3,600m. So, all the high-flying rhetoric about the dangers of playing at elevated levels, which are disputed in certain quarters, was effectively just hot air and the ban came back down to earth with a gasp.

488. BLANK LOOKS

Bradford City fans produced a book about rival Yorkshire club Leeds in late 2006.

Costing just £1, the 36-page paperback was entitled *Everything You Ever Wanted To Know About The Not So Massive Club That Was Super L666ds*.

Leeds supporters who snapped up copies as Xmas presents and settled down to read the contents found that it didn't take long – all 36 were blank.

489. IN THE DOGHOUSE

West Yorkshire police were in the doghouse after they banned Doncaster Rovers' mascot Donny the Dog, alias grandad Andy Liney, 58, from a March 2006 local derby.

Despite having written permission at appear at Huddersfield's Galpharm Stadium, Donny was intercepted by the police – 'I got within fifty yards of the stadium when I was stopped and told I was not going to be allowed in because of police intelligence,' he said.

Despite offering to remove his head and to sit in the stands Liney, mascot for five years, was told he could only enter the ground if he got changed into 'civvies'.

'The costume is an all-in-one double-lined fur suit so I don't wear anything underneath it, and I hadn't bought a change of clothes,' barked Donny who had to go walkies and spend the game on the supporters' coach.

Rovers chairman John Ryan threatened to report the police to the RSPCA but the constabulary's spokeswoman explained: 'The situation was risk-assessed, and based on the intelligence available a decision was taken not to allow the mascot on to the pitch before the match.'

And can't you just believe that they really think they were acting reasonably?

490. HURRY UP, BABE

The sensational transfer of England striker Jimmy Greaves for a record £80,000 from Chelsea to AC Milan in 1961 was nearly over before it began – when Jimmy's new baby refused to arrive on time.

For Greaves was due to join the Italian club on July 17 but said he would not travel to Milan until his second child, who had been due on July 15, was born.

When Milan heard this they 'showed a great sense of understanding by threatening to fine me £50 for every day I failed to make an appearance,' said Greaves.

The baby eventually arrived on August 8, and Greaves arrived in Milan on August 12 – resigned to a fine of £1,150.

491. SEX AND DRUGS AND KEVIN KEEGAN ...

En route to play against Yugoslavia and waiting for the flight at Belgrade Airport in June 1974, Kevin Keegan and Liverpool teammate Alec Lindsay were clowning around to kill time before going through passport control when two airport security guards suddenly grabbed Keegan, wrestled him to the ground, and hauled him away from the squad.

'They knocked me to the floor and dragged me into a small office where they thumped me around as if I was an international drug runner,' recalled Keegan.

It got worse: 'They made me kneel on the floor while accusing me of sexually assaulting one of the airline hostesses on the flight from Sofia, assaulting an airport guard, disturbing the peace and causing an obstruction.'

Outside, England boss Joe Mercer, with FA chairman Sir Andrew Stephen and secretary Ted Croker argued, demanded and pleaded for Keegan's release for an hour before he was reluctantly freed. 'I had a bloody nose and several bruises as proof of the brutal way the guards had manhandled me,' Keegan added.

Incredibly, Keegan and the squad went on with their tour, playing Yugoslavia in what was Mercer's last of seven games in charge and drawing 2-2 – with Keegan taking 'great satisfaction' from scoring the second.

492. IN THE RED, WITHOUT A TOUCH

1978 Kilmarnock signing Bobby Houston was on the bench for a game against his old side, Partick Thistle, who, as an intended joke, had wound him up pre-match by refusing to speak to him.

Houston, still on edge because of his reception and his relegation to substitute, was brought on in the second half, and as he passed Thistle boss Bertie Auld made a remark to him that only added fuel to the fire, before immediately making a lunge at Partick's Whittaker which missed its target.

Houston's former teammate Ian Gibson was outraged and shouted at the perpetrator, who promptly took a swing at him – missing again. Gibson then taunted Houston, who had another go at him before the referee and one of his linesmen intervened and sent Houston – who had not even made contact with the ball – off the pitch.

493. WE ONLY ASKED!

Preparing for their role in the Nigeria versus Gold Coast game in November 1955, Godwin Ironkwe and Peter Anieke were overheard by officials asking whether they were to receive a fee for playing. They were immediately suspended.

494. DROPPED!

When I played for, managed and was chairman of Hatch End FC in my younger days I once had a slight disagreement with George Mowle, former stalwart full-back for Wealdstone FC in the early '60s (19, not 18) and a very defensive manager of Hatch End Firsts, who I genuinely believe was happier with a 0-0 draw than a 5-4 win.

George was short of forwards one week and took reserve team striker Barry Jenkins to play for the Ones. They promptly won 3-0 with Jenkins notching all three goals on his debut. Next week he was dropped.

Stunned, I asked George why he had left Jenkins out. 'George, the lad scored a hat-trick.' 'Yes,' agreed George, puffing ruminatively on his beloved pipe and patting down his immaculately brylcreemed hair, 'but what ELSE did he do?'

I suspect George would have approved of Stockport County manager Lincoln Hyde, while Jenkins would have empathised with Frank 'Bonzo' Newton.

During the 1929-30 season, Newton was putting opposition Third Division North defences to the sword. In the opening 22 games of the season Newton, whose career record would eventually be 192 goals in 209 appearances, had hammered 21 goals.

Hyde dropped him.

But perhaps the striker's hard-luck tale to beat them all concerned Scotland's Henry Morris, drafted into attack from East Fife, aged 30, for the British International Championship game against Northern Ireland in 1949. He scored a hat-trick on his debut in the 8-2 triumph. The next game was against Wales, 39 days later – and Morris was discarded, never to figure again for his country.

495. BLIND LOYALTY

Steve Cook, from Welshpool, mid-Wales, travelled hundreds of miles every week to support Torquay United during the 1990s, but the 30-year-old audio typist revealed in April 1994 that he believed the hundreds of pounds he was spending was 'money well spent' despite being unable to see any of the matches as he is blind.

Devon-born Steve's friends, who accompany him to games, gave him a running commentary on the matches.

496. YOU'RE NOT KIDDING, JOE

Scottish international Joseph Cassidy played in all four home countries during his career from 1913 to 1932 – for Celtic, Bolton, Cardiff and Ballymena among others – and his four eldest children were born in Scotland, England, Wales and Ireland.

497. CROSSING THE LINE

Following four successive defeats, players at Italian Third Division club Viterbese were shocked to discover 11 wooden crosses, each bearing the name of a different player, planted in the middle of their pitch in January 1997.

The stunt had the desired effect and the team beat Juveterranova of Sicily next time out by 1-0, but skipper Massimiliano commented: 'We played with death in our hearts.'

498. GETTING THE BOOT BEFORE SIGNING

Third Lanark centre-half John Auld got the boot even before he played for his new club Sunderland in 1889 – for the shoemaker demanded as part of his transfer fee that his new club establish for him a boot and shoe business as well as giving him £20 for turning pro and then paying him £300 over the next two years.

499. PAYING THE PENALTY

Hearts' defender James Adams punched an opponent's shot away from his side's goal during an 1890-91 cup tie – protests about which action persuaded the Scottish FA to introduce penalty kicks.

The first penalty kick awarded against Hearts was conceded by their defender, er, James Adams, who later moved to the States where he became a sculptor.

500. CORPSE NAPPER

The body of former Nigerian soccer skipper Sam 'Zagallo' Opone was held to ransom by the witch doctor who had been treating him, as he claimed he had not been paid for his services.

Opone was treated by Blacky Awomni after he suffered a stroke in 1999 that left him paralysed.

When no money was forthcoming from family to pay for Awomni's care, the healer ceased treatment and the former defender died, reported the *Daily Telegraph*.

In April 2001 Awomni was still chasing payment, and seemed to have resorted to drastic tactics to get his cash. Former Nigerian FA official Austin Akosa was reported as saying: 'The herbalist has threatened the player's son that he will use magic to kill him if he does not come up with the money.'

Opone's son Lucky (!) protested: 'I'm yet to see my father's corpse, having only read about his death in the newspapers.'

AND FINALLY ...

So, you've had 500 stories. I hope you will indulge me for one more, about the football club closest to my heart than any other which, while I was writing this book, was enduring one of, if not the, toughest of times in even its chequered existence – Luton Town.

A period of ten-point deduction for going into administration included a surreal situation when manager Kevin Blackwell announced that he had resigned and would be leaving after the February 9 home game with Bournemouth, only to be sacked a week later along with his staff. He left complaining: 'We found out that Luton Town did not do what it said on the tin.' As a self-proclaimed, long-standing fan, he must have known that.

He also seemed to have turned into a parody of Margaret Thatcher and Queen Victoria when he stated in his resignation speech: 'We are announcing that we are leaving Luton Town.'

The points deduction almost guaranteed relegation from League One, particularly when coupled with the actions of the appointed administrator, Brendan Guilfoyle, in flogging off a couple of the club's best players – leaving them with just one recognised central defender – and ensuring that their loanees were sent back to their clubs.

However, amidst all this doom and gloom, I came across this defiant, slightly derivative piece of work by fellow fan, Mark Ledsom, entitled *The Luton Lord's Prayer* (see over).

Eric Morecambe
Who art in heaven
Hallowed be thy name
Let the goals come
They can have one
So long as our boys get seven
Give us this day a win
And forgive us our indebtedness
As we forgive those who have netted against us (except Watford)
Lead us out of administration
And deliver us from Guilfoyle
For we loved the Eighties
The power and the glory,
For ever and ever,
LUTON!

BIBLIOGRAPHY

Allen, Matt. *Where Are They Now ?* Highdown, 2007

Baddiel, David & Skinner, Frank. *Fantasy Football Diary*. Little, Brown 1994.

Baker, Barry. *A Journal Of African Football*. Heart Books, 2001

Ball, Phil. *Morbo* (Sic). Wsc, 2001

Bellos, Alex. *Futebol*. Bloomsbury, 2002

Blows, Kirk/ Hogg, Tony. *Essential History Of West Ham United*. Headline 2000.

Cascarino, Tony. *Full Time*. Scribner, 2000

Craig, Jim. *Scotland's Sporting Curiosities*. Birlinn, 2005

Delaney, Terence. *The Footballer's Fireside Book*. Sbc, 1963

Foot, John. *Calcio*. 4th Estate, 2006

Goldblatt, David. *World Football Yearbook; 2002–3; 2004–5*. Dorling Kindersley, 2002; 2003.

Grayson, Edward. *Corinthians & Cricketers*. The Naldrett Press, 1955.

Greaves, Jimmy & Gutteridge, Reg. *Let's Be Honest.* Sportsmans Book Club, 1973

Hayes, Dean. *Craven Cottage Encyclopaedia*. Mainstream, 2000.

Hayes, Dean. *Stockport County A-z*. Sigma, 1998

Hayes, Dean. *South Wales Derbies*. Pwp, 2003

Hesse-Lichtenberger, Ulrich. *Tor!* Wsc, 2002

Hutchinson, Roger. *Into The Light*. Mainstream, 1999.

Jackman, Mike. *Essential History Of Blackburn Rovers.* Headline 2001.

James, Brian. *England V Scotland*. Sbc, 1969.

Joyce, Michael. *Football League Players' Records 1888–1939*. Soccer Data, 2002.

Keegan, Kevin; Giller, Norman. *The Seventies Revisited*. Lennard Queen Anne Press, 1994

Lamming, Douglas. *A Scottish Internationalists' Who's Who, 1872–1986*. Hutton Press, 1987

MacWilliam, Rab. *The European Cup*. Aurum, 2000.

McColl, Graham. *Illustrated History Of Aston Villa 1874-1998.* Hamlyn, 1998

Menary, Steve. *Outcasts! The Lands That Fifa Forgot*. Know The Score, 2007.

Mourant, Andrew. *Essential History Of Leeds United.* Headline, 2000.

Owen, Wendy. *Kicking Against Tradition.* Tempus, 2005

Randall, David. *Great Sporting Eccentrics*. Guild Publishing, 1985.

Rollin, Glenda; Rollin, Jack (Editors). *Rothmans Football Yearbook, 1995/6; 1999/2000; 2000/1; 2001/2; 2002/3*. Headline

Rollin, Glenda; Rollin, Jack (Editors). *Sky Sports Football Yearbook 2005/6: 2006/7*. Headline

Rollin, Jack & Barrett, Norman. *Telegraph Football Yearbook 86-87*. Telegraph, 1986

Rollin, Jack. *Guinness Book Of Soccer Facts & Feats*. Guinness, 1978

Ross, David. *The Roar Of The Crowd*. Argyll, 2005.

Saunders, Donald. *World Cup 1962*. Sbc, 1964

Seddon, Peter. *Football Talk*. Robson, 2004

Sharpe, Graham. *Free The Manchester United One*. Robson, 2003

Twydell, Dave. *Rejected Fc Of Scotland Vol 2*. Yore, 1993

Vignes, Spencer. *Lost In France*. Stadia, 2007

Watson, Mike with Watson, Matthew. *The Tannadice Encyclopaedia*. Mainstream, 1997

Williams, Jean. *A Beautiful Game*. Berg, 2007